HAITI

THE LIVING
PEARL

By Beverly Grondin

The cover is from an oil painting I bought
on the side of the road in Haiti.
It hangs in my office today.

Dedicated to:

My Lord, for allowing me to go.

Jack Grondin, my husband, with much love.
Thank you for all your support.

Madison and Moriah, my darling
granddaughters who will one day go into all
the world.

My friend, Betty Clark, who told me for
years, "You need to write a book." To
which my answer was, "Betty, I'm too busy
living it." Get ready, Betty, there is more to
come.

Victory Bible Institute (VBI) for sending us.

Dear Bob Kamholtz and his lovely Florida
writing group: Roberta, Adel, Eve, Susan,
Kitt, Ed, Bill, and some of our *newbies*
thank you so much. *A* special thanks to
Roberta Sappington for her insight and
editing, and Bill Serle, who also edited and
helped me with publishing.

TABLE OF CONTENTS

FLYING HIGH

No internet. No smart phones. A squatty black rotary phone nobly sat on a wobbly table in the corner but rarely rang.

Here we were on the magnificent blue-crystal Caribbean coast. Swatting at mosquitoes while sitting in-doors. Jack, my husband and I endured the attacks because we believed it unhealthy to spritz bug spray on our skin.

The sun was blistering hot, which we didn't mind, and though willing to work outside, there was nothing scheduled for us to do.

Sent from our Bible School for two and a half months as missionary trainees to help the local ministry here, we arrived, enthused and inspired to take on our assignment. We soon found that teaching an hour long Bible Class at three o'clock on

Wednesday's was pretty much the extent of our duties.

I'd rise in the morning, after listening to creatures scratching in the old battered dresser that held our towels and linens, to read my Bible and prepare class lessons. In the evening by cordless lanterns or sometimes candles, I wrote in my journal, incessantly smacking the flies and pests nipping at my legs. My mind often wandered off to the sounds of the street vendors barking out

Beverly arrives in Haiti

their wares for sale, while balancing them in baskets on their heads. The ever-rank stench of human waste and garbage overpowered the smell of the few dinners cooking over open fires outside our compound.

I truly wondered if I would have an impact in this strange land. Not the dream I had of miraculous, powerful meetings, with lives saved and healings enveloping us like manna from heaven. Instead, lots of naps and endless hours on the porch without a view.

Michelin, a tall graceful Haitian, who always smelled as though she just returned from a bath, came three times a day to fix our meals. She knew little English and we, of course, knew no Creole. We soon learned to tell her, "*Manje a Gou, Michelin*," with lots of smiles and nodding. "Good food!"

Paulo, one of the older boys from the orphanage, who studied English, often came by to chat. He told us Michelin's desire was to be a professional chef. She was a single mother. Her two teen children went to school in a town in the mountains and lived with their grandmother. Michelin sent all the money she made to her mother to care for them. Her intention was to attend a culinary school to increase her cooking skills so she could earn more.

The first day we arrived, Michelin wanted to bless us with American food. So at great cost to the budget we had paid for our two month stay, she had purchased imported Kellogg Cornflakes for breakfast and Oscar Meyer hot dogs for lunch.

Jack and I were pretty much vegetarians at the time. We had been looking forward to the tropical fruit supposedly ready-for-the-picking from trees in the yard. Poverty being rampant, however, any fruit-bearing trees were bare by morning, relieved of their bounty at night. No fresh fruit! And the hot dogs left over from lunch, we found recycled in our spaghetti dinner that evening.

Electricity was on two hours each morning around 2 or 3 a.m. The refrigerator door was left open at night so it would not sweat. Of course, our scratching little vermin left the chest of drawers and migrated to the chest in the kitchen to avail themselves of any fresh foods. I knew because when I helped wash the carrots for the next day's beans and rice stew, there were indentures of tiny little teeth marks around the edges. Ugh!

It reminded me of a story I once heard. First year missionary sees a fly in the soup: gags, shoves the soup away. Second year missionary sees a fly in the soup: flicks the fly out, finishes the soup. Third year missionary sees a fly in the soup, bows his head and says, "Thank you Lord for the protein."

The light bulb hanging from a single wire in the kitchen would suddenly pop on in the middle of the night. This let us know the current was flowing. One of us had to open the mosquito net, hop out of bed to flip the switch for the inverters. This consisted of six car batteries and a gadget nailed to the wall that captured the allotted electricity to later draw power.

My evening ritual was to rinse off under the trickle of cold water from the showerhead, run to the bed, tuck in the mosquito net edges, otherwise pesky parasites wheedle their way in, and hope to fall asleep before my body temperature rose to an unbearable level. No air, no fans, no breeze. So when the two a.m. light came on, I had to repeat the ritual.

Our first night, just after dozing off, Jack and I awakened to a woman shrieking out chilling screams in Creole that sounded in English like "I'm Blessed, I'm Blessed," this she did for hours. At first, I prayed for her because obviously she wasn't blessed. Later nights, tense and frazzled, I'd bind the devil off her, hoping to quiet her. One night, with the pillow wrapped around my ears, I desperately prayed for her *blessed* hormones to settle down, thinking maybe she was going through the change or something. I don't really know what stirred her up, but it nightly unnerved Jack and me.

But again that first night when peace was finely restored, I drifted back to sleep, only to be startled into a scene from Jurassic Park with sounds of a pack of screeching T-Rex. Our room shared a wall with the church next door, a shell of a concrete building with vents at the top to let the heat out. Later, we realized the cleaning ladies mopping the dust-crated surfaces, dragged the old wooden pews front to back across unfinished floors for the five a.m. Morning Prayer. It seemed to echo for miles.

Inactivity drained our days. A sigh of relief escaped one day, as I slipped away from the four rooms, fled the dark windowless kitchen and unlocked the barred door of the porch. I felt like a three-year old, suddenly loosed from its mother's hand, running free to venture around our concrete village.

The thick walls surrounding us had broken glass cemented to the top for protection. It looked like something from a gloomy ice castle, as the evening sun reflected off the jagged edges. The yard was completely concrete.

The boys' orphanage was on the other side of two mesh fences, their openings ajar. I caught the eye of the big burly guy at the gate, as I passed by the guard shack. He watched my every move. Rumor was, he had a sordid reputation and carried some pretty heavy fire power to protect us from any uninvited outsiders.

Some of the older boys, leaning against the building, nodded shyly. As I started up the stairs, I heard peals of laughter. I grabbed my required skirt around my legs and took a deep breath as I stepped over the opening past the metal door onto the roof. The younger boys flashed warm, friendly smiles my way. The very young rushed to give hugs. They were ripe from running and playing in the heat and the odor lingered on my skirt that night, but I didn't mind. This later became the place I loved to come to pray for Haiti, the boys, and the lives we were slowly touching.

I patted my heart, awestruck at these kids scrambling around the rooftop without supervision. Inching over to the ones huddling near the edge of the knee-high wall, I followed their gaze and realized, they were flying kites. Not big colorful types with infinite balls of twine and fancy tails, but kites made from candy wrappers, ragged pieces of paper or anything lightweight they could find. Shaped the size of a square greeting card, two small sticks crossed at the center were tied off through holes, leaving the thread trailing out from the middle. The string was not continuous but apparently collected one piece at a time found on the streets or plucked from their clothes. Tied end to end, you could see the small string-tails up the line as it unwound from the tiny twig in their hand.

The boys pulled to and fro on the string. I watched the kite-warriors dance and twirl as if readying for war. And war it was. All across the rooftops throughout Carrefour, the poorest section of an already poor nation, children were flying their crude kites doing battle with neighboring pilots. Up and down and over they flew, attacking, swirling, to cause the opponent to fall or to tangle on clotheslines or the few electrical wires between houses. Our guys were experts and we were winning.

Mackenzie, bright and cheerful, with a grin of white teeth that seemed too big for his mouth, turned to me and without words, told me to take over, as he tried to hand me the string. At first, I backed away fearing I would lose, perhaps, his only treasure. But at his insistence, I took the reins.

I experienced a rush of happiness, the fragile paper rising higher and higher. Some of the boys danced around me, as I dipped and swirled, making defensive moves away from our rivals.

I'd like to say I won the battle for us that night, but suffice it to say, I didn't lose the kite. General Mackenzie took us on to victory. What I did gain however, was their respect.

BALEK

Joel, at the guard shack, opened the gate as the blue truck rumbled into the compound. We had finally asked his name, which erased some of the mystery around him. Underneath the gruff exterior was a kind man, watching over us like a guardian angel. We tossed him a friendly wave as his eyes followed us. We hastened toward the big truck, hoping for a ride, longing to see more of Haiti.

I remembered Balek, our lanky, round-faced driver with serious dark eyes, from the Port au Prince Airport.

I shiver recalling the intimidating police officer that took away Balek's license, only two weeks before, for parking in a pickup zone to load our luggage.

We nearly caused an uprising with unofficial "helpers" who hovered outside the airport to assist with suitcases for arrivals. Helper's rule: If I *touch* your bag, I get a tip.

We politely swished our hands out in front of us, as we blurted, "No, no thank you, please it's okay, we can do it, no..." Compassion poured from my heart for these men yet I hugged my purse a little tighter. My eyes shifted left then right as the fervor and tension continued to build. Horns honked, Haitians shouted in Creole and crowds were hustling to the parking lot.

I've said for a long time that God gave me a missionary nose, but even I was taken back by the foul smells that swarmed us. By the time we reached Balek, ten different hands had touched our bags and followed us over.

Jack breathed out, "Do you have any change? I only have large bills on me."

I mumbled a yes and a prayer...*thank you Lord, for protecting us all...* then poked around the bottom of my purse, as Jack dug into his pockets. We produced handfuls of nickels, dimes and quarters, between us amounting to about three or four dollars. Jack motioned to the leader-of-the-ten to share the cash with the others.

The unbathed, dirty gentleman got all twitchy as he stared at the coins then fitfully threw them into the back of Balek's truck. This agitated his "crew" and they joined him in yelling and fist pumping, resulting in a near riot! Frightening! Balek towering over them returned their barks. That was when Mr. Scary Cop showed up.

After a lot of spit flying, more shouts and threatening gestures, the mini-mob finally ran off. Balek was left with a ticket.

Marilyn, a portly, pretty, black woman from the States had come with Balek to retrieve us from the airport and served somewhat as an interpreter. The three of us quickly scrambled up into the back of Balek's truck and were locked in the cage that covered all but the cab.

Bouncing around unmercifully, Jack and I held on for dear life as Balek raced to catch up with the cop who took his license. We grabbed the bar above our heads to steady ourselves on the bolted-to-the-floor bench on the right, Marilyn in her 60+ years, rolled in giggles from the seat on the left.

"Watch your head," Jack shouted over the rattle and bump.

Our luggage repeatedly slid front to back. We stopped abruptly in front of a whitewashed shack and watched Balek run inside. No idea where we were or how long we would be here.

Marilyn's tone turned serious, "In Haiti, if the police take your license and you don't know which station they took it to, you could be without permission to drive for months until you get it back. Balek makes his living driving for the ministry."

We all nodded.

Gathering my wits about me, I asked, "Marilyn, where are you from?"

She answered, "I am a retired nurse of 25 years, originally from Nashville, Tennessee. I was sent from your same Bible School. I arrived three months ago and work with the ministry in Lamentin. You will be working in Carrefour."

My muscles relaxed and my breathing calmed as I listened to her chatter about the mishaps of *her* arrival in Haiti.

Within the hour, Balek came out. He shoved his license into the front pocket of his bright yellow shirt, cranked the motor and took off like a maniac to the base.

We zoomed around traffic, and he incessantly blew his horn. I thought he was still upset, but as we jostled around in every direction, like popcorn in a hot air popper, Marilyn assured us he always drove that way.

Now, two weeks later, Balek had returned to the base. He leaped from the cab and followed the aroma, of Michelin's beans and rice and spicy chicken, flowing from the kitchen. By the time we caught up to him, he was leaning on the wall, with one foot propped up, shoveling in a spoonful of rice from his plate. He had come to pick up money. When we heard he was going for supplies, we hand-motioned that we wanted to go with him. Risky! But we were hungry to take a break from the concrete kingdom and see some sights.

We crawled up front into the cab, this time hoping to take pictures to preserve our journey. Jack and I grinned at each other, then braced ourselves. We pulled our backpacks and water bottles firmly onto our laps and waved once more to Joel, as we cleared the gate.

There was one main road to town. It was paved but stayed tangled with traffic like a pile of clothes hangers. Balek preferred to travel the rocky side roads. Not gravel-rock but full size rock as big as grapefruit. He thought nothing of driving onto the sidewalk to dodge the many TapTaps.

TapTap, typically, is a small pickup with a topper on the bed. The area inside the back has benches on each side much like Balek's truck, designed to haul people. Public transportation... Their charm is the bright colors of green, yellow, and red flowers, palms, and local scenes hand painted over the entire vehicle. They're called TapTap because a tap on the side of the truck signals the driver to let you on or off.

Riding with Balek one day, Jack and I both stomped the floor, as Balek rolled onto the sidewalk, nearly hitting an elderly lady. She dove into the next stall in time to get out of his way. Instead of remorse, I watched Balek laugh.

THE PEARL

Jostling along in Balek's truck, I thought back to the day we first flew over Haiti, once known as the Pearl of the Antilles.

In its' boom, the Pearl received cruise ships and Love Boats bearing passengers to experience the splendor of the exotic Caribbean shores. Now, a clear dividing line existed between two very distinct countries, the Dominican Republic and Haiti.

Flying over the Dominican side, I recall seeing lush green palms bowing a welcome like white-gloved butlers. Freshly painted houses in pastel pink, tangerine, and aqua blues, the color of an early morning sky, formed a reception line of hospitality. Flowery hillsides melted into sandy white beaches inviting visitors to come rest by the clear still waters. Webs of roads laid paths to untamed tropical sights or shuttled a traveler to one of its fine restaurants. In harmony, the hotels nested along the shoreline, with doors swung wide, like open arms ready to embrace the lodger, all the while, supplying provision for its own Dominican families.

As the airplane banked left, details of Haiti and the horseshoe shaped island, became visible. By contrast, it was dark, barren, backward and if not for the precious souls there, repelling. Small barren villages clustered in sparse groves of banana trees scattered over the countryside. No new plantings, only charred fields, light vegetation, and murky waters. The once lavish trees and wooded areas had been felled and burned to provide cooking fuel for a starving people.

Continuing through town, Jack had snapped hazy photos through the windshield of Balek's truck. Finally, Jack hand-cranked the window down in order to capture a clearer shot of the city. Shacks made of concrete, salvaged cloth, paper, plastic, and tin were cleverly pieced together to create a house but still looked like cardboard boxes crammed behind a grocery store, waiting to be demolished. Jack got *the eye* from Balek, which meant close the window. He liked his air conditioning!

Wars, selfish dictators, corrupt use of tax money brought the Pearl's former beauty to ruin. It seems she's been unable to recover to this day. Some say the Haitian people made a pact with the devil.

The women had black satin skin and short cropped hair and though their countenance was often sad, they were beautiful. Both men and women glided down the street, in a way Jack and I lovingly refer to as *the Haitian walk*. It's a suave, smooth rowing motion of swinging arms and legs flowing in a gentle rhythmic sway as if a cool jazz piece was endlessly playing in their heads. They were poor, but they held themselves upright with the dignity of a monarch.

Our vehicle continually bounced along the streets, and I watched hard-working people eke out a living in ingenious ways. Shirtless men, muscles bulging, glistened with sweat as they painstakingly pushed hand-made carts heaped high with stacks of blocks or tires, furniture, or several 100 lb. bags of beans and rice. They were the ox to the carts, crafted from scrap wood and metal that laboriously rolled on two hijacked bicycle tires.

Many men, women, and children balanced baskets of homemade breads, *papitas* or other foods on their heads. Suddenly I poked my husband and gasped, "Look! It's unbelievable." Balek laughed out loud.

Jack swung the camera around in the direction I pointed. A woman in a mismatched skirt and blouse walked suavely down the road, balancing a five gallon, sturdy white bucket full of water on her head. Not a drop was lost.

Our chauffeur slowed alongside a young boy, his palm-leaf basket packed with 30 or 40 small tied plastic bags with a tiny straw inserted in the middle. Ice cold drinking water! Balek purchased a couple of bags for himself and looked over at us. We both shook our heads at the same time. He rolled up his window then sped off as the boy rapidly called out to other cars, "*Dlo, dlo, dlo.*"

Stopped in traffic, Balek opened his window this time for *papitas*, crispy fried banana slices. He glanced our way and we instantly nodded yes. Clean? Umm, questionable! Greasy! Salty! Yes, and delicious!

After a stop for the orphanage's supplies of beans and rice, we continued to the Culligan plant for fresh water. Jack took a photo of a common sight: elderly men chipping large chunks of ice out of rusty freezer chests as old as they were. The frozen water was suspiciously cloudy.

Dotted along the streets were vendor stalls made of stick posts and blue plastic or tattered cloths canopied over peddlers and their wares, screening the pulsing sunrays. I caught a glimpse of a young mother openly nursing her unclothed infant behind rows of dusty motor oil and transmission fluid bottles.

In the booth beside her, a young male walked back and forth in his open air drug-store, sparsely stocked with toothpaste, soaps, lotions, shampoos and various items. Lord knows, how long an old beat-up Corolla, jacked up on rocks nearby, had been waiting for a part or tire change. A poor man's Firestone…

A tiny trader perched on an overturned bucket, cooking meat strips over an open fire in a cut-off metal barrel. Smelled like chicken, probably tasted like chicken. But riding through town, I noticed very few dogs or cats roaming about.

And there was the ever present pile of garbage raked in front of each place. Flies buzzing. The stench hung so strong in the air, it wafted up through the truck, though the windows were closed in the air conditioned cab.

But the most overpowering thing to see was knee-high boys and girls, too young to be away from the watchful eye of a doting mother, standing in the middle of this dreadful traffic. Balancing on narrow street dividers, they waved at cars, begging for money.

Tears stung my eyes and my throat closed watching these tiny little girls with matted eyes and hair. Their soiled dresses of wilted lace hung loose on their frail dark bodies.

Daniel, from the orphanage, had told us earlier that these barely-past-toddler street daughters were often pimped out. Doing things spoken of only in the dark. *Tragic! Horrible!* Yet reality? This often meant the difference between whether her family ate a meal that day or not.

My mother-heart broke. I silently screamed, *Empty your pockets, go buy food, take them home with you...* I longed to bathe them, to untangle and shampoo their hair and intertwine ribbons into their braids to match a new dress and sparkle shoes. Then at the end of the day to put a fresh nightgown on them and one by one rock them to sleep, giving them a night's rest without fear, hunger, or danger.

A sudden halting jerk! We were at the water store. A crew loaded water jugs into the back of the truck.

Jack and I quickly scrambled out of the cab and ran toward the street babies. As they crossed the road, they dodged cars running to greet us.

In my mind, it somehow seemed wrong to take their pictures, but like runway models, each one struck a pose. Everyone giggled and grinned, posturing for position, then huddle hugged each other like old army buddies. Soon they wrapped themselves around my legs holding tight. I paused, whispering a prayer over each precious head, sensing that they felt safe, if only for a moment.

Ever aware of their own great need, they encircled us both and held out their dirty dimpled hands, expecting to be paid.

Somehow we *have to show people what is happening here. Quick Jack, snap the shot.*

VITA MOSQUITO

One morning Jack and I woke covered in welts, as if our grandkids had dotted our bodies in the night with red markers. The mosquitos were especially bad after the rains and they had feasted at our expense.

We presented ourselves to Michelin at breakfast, miming and talking loud describing our need for a mosquito net.

After breakfast, I had just set my coffee cup in its saucer when a tall thick-set young woman stepped lively onto the porch. In perfect English and a sing song voice, she sang, "Good Morning, I'm Vita."

One look at us and she exclaimed, "Oh my, Michelin said you had many bites."

Scratching our arms and legs, relieved to speak English, we introduced ourselves then repeated our desire for a net.

"Do you have Haitian money, gourdes?" she asked, "We will need a large mosquito net for your bed and it will probably cost around $4.00 USD.

"That would be great Vita, thank you," I said.

"I know just the place. Are you ready to go?"

"Oh yeah, we'll be right back.

Jack and I, already dressed, collected a few things for the backpack. Without consciously thinking about it, we followed Vita outside the gate. We had only just met her and yet we trailed behind her, doing whatever she told us to do.

My trust is in You Lord. Your
Ways are larger than Vita and I know You are
guiding us.
You brought us to Haiti, I know You can
protect us!

We tiptoed down the long street in front of the orphanage, trying to avoid the nasty mud that caked our shoes. Without my summer tan, I'm sure my very pale skin and blonde hair drew the neighbors' attention. I noticed several peek from the doors of the row houses, but none waved.

Vita turned the corner onto a busy road. A brightly colored small pickup truck slowed alongside of us, and Vita's long arm reached over to smack the side of the truck. It stopped and she motioned for us to crawl in the back.

Pausing before the mouth of the truck topper at the rear, I stared at thirty sets of eyes blinking back at me. There was nowhere to sit. As large as Vita was and the two of us, I had my doubts this would be our taxi to town. Magically, Vita entered the small dark tunnel and sat next to an elderly woman with two bags in her lap. Jack helped me aboard. I sat next to an old man, hoping I wasn't crushing him, as Jack settled beside me. Off we went, in our first ride in a TapTap.

A famous Haitian joke asks, "How many Haitian's can you get in a TapTap?" Answer: "Always one more."

There was no personal space, and my bubble was continually invaded. We were shoulder to shoulder everywhere we went. But my thoughts were smiling at our wee adventure.

Tapping from the inside notified the driver that someone wanted off. Taps from the outside meant someone wanted on. It was start and stop all the way to the market. Around 45 minutes later, Vita whacked the inside of the pickup and it stopped abruptly. She quickly hustled us off, handing some coins to a man sitting in the passenger's seat.

I loved the market place. The sounds of vendors calling your attention to their stall, the smells of new leather purses, wallets thrown in piles, shoes in random sizes strung from wire racks, and the wonderful food smells, but most of all, I loved catching a glimpse of these people's lives.

The stalls were jammed together, topped with cloth so tightly bunched that it blocked the sunlight. I didn't dare look around too much. Vita moved swiftly down narrow footpaths through the market and I didn't want to lose her.

Suddenly something got between Jack and me. I stumbled to the left. A wiry man in stained clothing shoved forward what looked like a cart, parting the crowd like an icebreaker ship. I gasped, when I realized sloshing around in his wheel barrow was the head, body and legs of a chopped goat, floating in its own blood.

I braced myself against a pole to avoid falling into the lap of the stall owner next to me. Jack reached across and grabbed my arm.

Life, all life, was so fragile in this country.

We both shook our heads, then desperately craned our necks to find Vita.

Thank you Lord, Vita is tall, I prayed, then spotted her red scarf. Jack and I hurried in her direction.

When we caught up to her, she was leaning over a large wooden table outside a shop, sorting through cellophane packages. She raised a yellow one in the air and said, "This will be just the right size. Do you have the money?" Jack dug in his pocket, handed her the gourdes we had and she paid for it, returning our change.

We retraced our steps through the crowded stands. I side-stepped a lady who stopped on the edge of the road and hiked her skirt to pee. Distracted by the idea that we were in the middle of town, I tore my skirt and a small piece of my leg on the bumper of a rusted flat-bed trailer.

Vita, ran into the street and slapped the side of a minivan about to pass us by. It had no side doors or hatch door. As it slowed, we jumped inside and sat across from a well-dressed little family.

Leaning back in the seat, I took Jack's hand. *Whew,* w*hat a morning!*

We were back in time for lunch. Vita disappeared before we could invite her to eat, but Jack and I only had a little time before our afternoon class. I changed my skirt and put antiseptic on my leg, then we gathered our lessons and dashed to class.

When we returned, we walked our things back to our room. Yellow netting swung freely from bent, 16p nails on the ceiling, like a royal canopy over a princess' bed. A few concrete chips splattered the top of our sheets.

Vita had spent the day taking care of us. She knew we would sleep better that night but didn't stay for a thank you.

BROTHER TIM

Jack and I relaxed into the quiet routine of our base. Marilyn came over on Sundays to go to church with us and we enjoyed a time of English-speaking fellowship.

One particular Sunday after dinner, she said, "You know ya'll are getting a roommate don't cha? We're going to the airport tomorrow to pick him up. You want to go?" Before she could take a vote, we simultaneously chimed, "Yes," our usual answer to do-you-want-to-go-anywhere.

Tim was a beefy, balding fireball. His skin was translucent and never tanned, except his face and thick neck which stayed a constant blush, brightened by the heat. He didn't ask Balek, but hopped in the front cab alongside him, while the rest of us headed back to the cage.

Tim didn't lack for words and brought our porch to life with tales of the miracles God had worked as he preached around the southern states.

We swapped stories and laughed a lot. Mostly at our own inadequacies. But also at how God used us in spite of us. This man's faith was strong and he believed God would do most anything he prayed.

Tim settled in the room across the hall from ours, he had his own bathroom. Once he unloaded his bags he called out, "Hey ya'll, come over here for a minute."

To our amazement, he opened a duffle bag solely dedicated to nothing but good ole American junk foods: candy bars, tootsie rolls, Reese's Pieces, cookies, Pringles, Little Debbie's, white powdered donuts and the like. We smiled, but in time assured

him that we were more into healthy foods. We had long talks on the porch about it. But occasionally, we indulged in his goodies, only to encourage our brother that we were a team, of course.

That night, Tim was introduced to "I'm

Blessed, I'm Blessed". We heard him framming around in the kitchen once our little Jurassic Park started. His first words after good morning, "We have got to find that screaming woman and pray for her. Lord, have mercy, she was up all night. How in the world have you stood it? Plus, I'm going to need a mosquito net." The swollen bites looked like measles and intensified his ruddy face.

Pastor F, the director of the Bible school, came by early and told Tim he had two classes a week to teach and would be called on to preach at the Thursday night services. Tim's reputation preceded him, and this bold preaching machine was asked to expound often. His North Carolina twang gave the interpreter a little trouble, but the enthusiasm he exuded from the platform was easily understood. The people loved him.

Some of the VBI students pleaded with us to teach them English. After we cleared it with the director, Jack and I put a curriculum together to teach them basic phrases and numbers. We used materials from ESL (English as a Second Language) and pulled pages from a few coloring books we brought: pictures of airplanes, boats, trains, and cars. Four or five pupils already knew a little English. They loved to practice their skill between classes.

We had many laughs together as they struggled to repeat words that started with TH. Their pink tongues would curl like one of Tim's tootsie rolls, still only producing the T sound. "Through" was my favorite word stumper. Their faces contorted and twisted trying to find what combination it took to pronounce THR.

One Day, standing at the front of the class teaching on Faith, I felt a flood of what looked like a liquid capital L flowing straight down from heaven and out from me to those sweet faces in front of me. PURE LOVE! Precious souls… In that moment, I actually felt God's immense love for these young men and women.

In the same instance, I felt something wasn't quite right. Jack took over teaching. As I became less aware of myself and more aware of them, I noticed some of our students were drowsy, almost dizzy-like in their seats. As I strolled around the class, I prayed, "*Lord, show us what they need from us. Help us to be sensitive to Your desire for them.*" One by one, I softly patted each of their backs. They would stir and sit a little taller then melt in a slump as I passed.

During break time, I asked Paolo, who interpreted for us, "Do you think they are enjoying the class? Maybe it's too much being taught in English all the time."

Paolo immediately responded, "Oh no, please. They love the classes. They talk about it all the time. They especially love Mr. Jack and you, Madam Jack." A customary address for the wife.

"Then what is going on with them? I can sense something?"

Paolo dropped his head and whispered, "I'm sorry to say, Madam Jack. Most of them come from great distances. They spend their money on TapTap rather than food. Many have not eaten, sometimes for days."

I nearly crumpled to the ground, stricken! *Lord, how did we not know this*?

I rushed over to Jack, excused myself to Jonathan, the student talking English with him, and relayed what Paolo had said.

Jack raced back to our quarters to find Tim. Between the two of them, they pulled enough gourdes (Haitian money) together to send Thomas, from the orphanage, for a case of ice cold Tampico (a favorite bottled fruit drink) and papitas from the street vendors. Tim brought cookies from his stash.

We refreshed ourselves together, thankful that we found out what was happening. Our treasured students got much needed food and we knew we were hearing from God.

Oh Lord, You are so Faithful.

LIGHT OF THE WORLD

Music! A universal language.

Worship music. Songs to be sung to the Lord. David, the Biblical young shepherd boy, understood worship and was later called a man after God's own heart, for he praised in the cool of the night, soothing his sheep by the sound of his singing. He fought lions and bears, and even a giant once. Yet, this child, who loved his Shepherd, understood the power of music.

I grew up in church singing in the choir and playing parts in the holiday musicals. We studied the lives of hymn writers, as well as the missionary stories of men and women going off to places barely known, overcoming extreme conditions.

My Jack, however, was fairly new to the idea of missions. And now, he was living on the field in a foreign country. Away from creature comforts in the middle of a risky, life-threatening habitat.

He had been a professional musician in a rock and roll band, *38 Special,* for 18 years. Along with notoriety came years of alcohol, drug use, or what he calls, "the devil's playground of, druggin', drinkin', smokin', cussin', chasin'."

I never knew that man. I only know Jack as a man of God. And with God's help, those things had fallen off by the time we met. But music! Well, it was still so much a part of him. And like David, he loves to worship.

But after days of brooding, he finally lamented, "I feel invisible…looking for where I fit, where I belong. It's okay teaching in the Bible school. You love it! But my heart is not satisfied here."

Not much I could say in the moment, so I waited and prayed.

Lord, my husband needs to know the hope of his calling and to know that he is vital here. He longs for a way to fully express his love for You that fills that longing. He wants to know he is making a difference in Haiti.

Late one afternoon, I headed for the rooftop; it was time for the Kite Games with the boys. Tim, who was called often to preach was in his room studying.

Jack followed the sound of music across the compound and entered the church next door. Musicians were doing a sound check, as the singers set up for rehearsal. They were a handsome group of young men and women, late teens to twenties, with a heart-warming blend of vocal sounds. They called themselves *Light of the World*. That day, they lit Jack's world.

Thank you, Lord!

These kids came together from around the community and had formed a group, and the group cleaved to Jack.

Soon after their connection with Jack, they streamed by in the evenings to hang out on our porch, like in an old Andy Griffin Show. One evening, after a hardy round of singing, they each leaned forward to listen as my husband opened his heart to share with them the pitfalls of being in the limelight. Tim grabbed a chair, and joined us. Daniel, whose girlfriend was a member of the group, interpreted.

Jack sat, resting his arms on his legs and holding his hands open in front of him. Gently he said, "Fame, fortune, and the world at my fingertips. It did not bring fulfillment. I tried many things. Looking for love in all the wrong places. The things of this world can never quench that thirst."

He continued, "Fame has the greatest pull. It causes pride in your mind and is difficult to remove. It continually raises its head. To this day, while standing on a platform singing to the Lord, my past shouts in my mind, 'Look, they think you are really good.' But instead, I quickly look to the Lord, telling Him that He is my God and there is no other. He helps me to stop the thoughts. Believe me, loving God, and knowing His love is what fills the void and satisfies the longings."

Sitting in the quiet afterward, a foot tapped, a hum purred, and suddenly our hearts poured out into a crescendo of song. The Presence of God charged the atmosphere. I felt electrified, as if I'd stuck a wet finger on the car batteries of the inverter.

Apparently, I was not alone because no one moved, as a hush reclaimed the room. One by one, each person reverently left us and wandered out past the gate.

Tim, Jack and I sat glued to our chairs. Content, I barely breathed.

Thank you, thank you Lord most high
In Your presence, oh Lord is fullness of joy.
Joy unspeakable and full of glory. Your
Peace is beyond understanding.

More and more, Light of the World's visits became the norm. I offered to direct the group. They were inspired learners. In spite of broken keys and un-tuned instruments, their expression of love developed into synched voices of heavenly harmony. The adolescents brought a snare, bass, and high hat to assemble together for Jack. With Paolo on a small keyboard and Jack on drums, we played and sang together for hours.

They were still awestruck by the celebrity, Jack. A couple of them used treasured money to look him up on the internet, at the local Cyber Café.

The café, which we visited later, consisted of a dirty dilapidated shed with outdated computers under a table made from an old flat door resting on cinder blocks. It was stuffy and smelled of hot wires. I sat in front of the bulky white screen to check our email, as Jack paid ten gourdes ($1) for an hour. My fingers hesitated over the top of the smeared keyboard, unsure what was dried on it. Nasty!

After practicing several weeks on the porch with *Light of the World*, Jack and I awoke early one Sunday to a loud rap on the door and someone calling out to us.

Bleary-eyed, Jack opened the door to encounter the tall, broad shouldered Bishop J. He was lighter skinned than most of his peers, and had been raised in the mountains of Haiti. This humble minister oversaw many of the churches in the area and exuded an unseen power that brought great respect.

Taking my husband's hand, he declared,

"Brudder Jack, you are preaching in the service this morning. I will see you at the church in *one* hour."

Breathe Brudder Jack, breathe.

"JURASSIC PARK" CHURCH

"JURASSIC PARK" CHURCH

Jack isolated himself in a backroom. He had an hour to prepare to preach at *Jurassic Park* church. We lovingly nicknamed it that because of the early morning scraping of the pews.

We stepped inside the church building made of solid masonry, ceiling to floor. Horizontal slat vents, completely concrete, circled the tops of the walls to allow the heat to escape and a breeze in. No other windows and only two entryways with one small backdoor. Perfect architecture for the climate.

I sat quietly before the service, fascinated by the decorations. All walls were painted a pastel green. Bunches of simple, sweet red flowers tied together adorned the tall white pillars, like the ribbon-draped Maypole we danced around as children. Small patches of flowers, yellow and white, but mostly red, hung on threads in clumps, dangling from the ceiling throughout the sanctuary. I never touched them to see if they were real.

Local greenery shooting out of colorful, hand-painted clay pots lined the platform, four feet off the ground. As I looked up from the front row bench, my head tilted back so far that my mouth naturally fell open giving me a look of one in great awe or one, a breath away from a snore. Since Jack was preaching, I hoped he'd know I was in 'awe.'

In the tradition of *Jurassic Park* church, the women wore long dresses, were not adorned with makeup or jewelry and covered their heads. Some ladies had elaborate lace scarves, others wore hats, or laid a scrap of cloth on their head to be proper. I had worn my hat before, and shivered at the trickles of moisture running down my back. In the market, I found a lace doily for a few gourdes. In a small moment of panic, I reached for the tiny white doily on top of my head and remembered the two bobby pins holding it in place.

I thought good missionary ladies should dress modestly so as not to embarrass their community. Therefore, I wore long denim skirts, soft-colored blouses, and a straw hat. Amazingly, the congregation, as poor as they were, dressed far better than I had come prepared to dress. Earlier, I noticed when they arrived outside the church, they stopped to wipe their shoes clean and tidy themselves and their children before entering. It was beyond me how the men wore freshly laundered, pressed shirts with ties and belted pants. Those who did not were frowned upon.

Exuberant, lively singing and clapping were accompanied by unskilled musicians. The congregation didn't seem to mind the loud, out-of-tune guitars, off-beat drums and keyboards with missing keys. However, there was no denying the players' reverent devotion and desire to serve God.

Worship lasted at least an hour. My hair stood on end, as the church sang in a language I did not know, yet knowing the One to whom they sang. It was chilling. My thoughts were interrupted when I realized the 'pine sol' clean smell had faded and was replaced by the now sweaty crowd.

An elder stood, dwarfed by the massive old wood podium. Our interpreter said that the elder had asked, "Would all visitors please stand and introduce yourself and tell us why you have come today." I felt embarrassed for an unkempt gentleman who rose. Mentally, I wrapped my arms over his slumped shoulders, as he bowed his head to give his name. "Albert."

To my horror, the head elder's eyes stared hard as a diamond, then asked, "Albert, are you saved?" Albert, not looking up, swung his head left to right. Suddenly the elders swarmed to pray for him, a custom I can't imagine anyone tolerating, much less creating a desire to return. My eyes followed the elders as one by one they hovered over each standing guest, like bees to a field of flowers. We continued to sing, softly, until the elders returned to the platform.

After two hours of worship, prayers, and announcements, Jack was introduced and invited forward to give the day's message. My attention now diverted to him, I felt proud as he bravely preached through an interpreter about Abraham, his favorite Bible person. Abraham had great faith and spoke directly to God. Jack encouraged us to have that kind of faith, a personal relationship in dialogue with God.

Without warning, in the middle of his message, the lights went out. The electric oscillating fans, fastened high in the corners, whirred to a stop. The car batteries of the inverter had worn down from the long service. Silence and darkness overpowered the moment. Out of the shadows, a generator growled a dreadful noise like a beast. Overhead lights flickered while the rickety fans of *Jurassic Park* church whined back to life. Jack resumed preaching. I barely heard the Amen over the racket.

Lord, someone painted You as a hard taskmaster, demanding and overbearing.

I pray, Lord, Jurassic Park church comes to know Your Grace and love for them.

THE MOUNTAIN TRIP

The mission base was buzzing. Balek and some of the boys hoisted several large crates overhead to the truck bed. A large, empty, cylinder-like black tub, used to hold water on top of a building, was being tied atop the blue truck.

Something was up. Tim walked into the middle of the chaos to ask what was going on. He returned to the porch, where Jack and I stood watching and in a loud tone said, "Hey, we're going to the mountains. We are invited, so better grab your stuff. We leave at noon. "

Heading back to our room to pack, I noticed Michelin and Beatrice in the kitchen. Steaming pots of rice on the stove and large containers of chicken parts scattered over the counter top. They had already been busy cooking. Looked like we would have lots of mouths to feed on the road.

The last of the crates and several of the older boys were already loaded when we returned to the truck. Paolo, Daniel, and Obed came along, prepared to interpret. My bulging backpack hanging over my shoulder, I paused wondering where we should stow our gear and where we would sit. True to the cultural norm, "there's always room for one more", we scrunched into the truck.

Jack and I wrangled our way in to the left side, my backpack settled on my lap. Even Joel, the guard, moved over as Tim positioned himself next to us. No foot room, nothing to hold onto, and boys piled on top of crates hunched over, matching the arch of the ceiling. I wanted to holler, "Forward, Ho!" for some reason.

We barreled-off out of the gate and down the road, as Balek disregarded his cargo. I noticed two white ministry vehicles leading the way. Passing through town remarkably quickly, I wriggled left and right to see around Jack and the others, trying to take it all in. Jack rolled his eyes at me, but smiled.

It was muggy hot, the kind that takes your breath, refusing to fill your lungs, and it felt like we were all stuck together. The stench of the city still grabbed for my attention, but I loved being away from the base, experiencing new sights and seeing new people.

At last, we headed toward more of a rural route, with long stretches of grassless fields, and patches of thin banana trees, and small Lamentins (towns). After hours of riding, suddenly our caravan pulled to the side of the road, and we all piled out.

Mysteriously, Michelin appeared. Even more mysteriously, she pulled from somewhere beneath us, a set of stackable metal pots with a lid. Setting up her makeshift kitchen on the edge of the truck bed, she piled dollops of rice onto paper plates adding a piece of cooked chicken to each. It was still hot. Jack said he was starved. I was thankful for a plastic spoon, not complaining about lacking a napkin.

After a quick visit to the bushes, my husband standing guard for me, we were back on the road.

With a full belly and no talking over the noise, I lost myself in prayer and thoughts of God's plan and purpose for this trip to the mountains. Even after an hour's ride, there was still a measure of hot city smell that mingled with the local charred-out tree stumps, smoldering along the way. My guess - after harvesting the wood, these poor folks set fire to the center of the trees and cooked on the spot.

I was startled out of my thoughts when Balek abruptly turned a corner onto a dirt road, and I watched some of our guys pulling on coats, hats, scarves and hunkering down in the back of the truck. *It's 90 degrees out here. What is going on?*

This was no ordinary dirt road. Actually, it was a dusty, rocky, dried-up river bed. A short cut! Hmmm.

Dust rolled in like ocean waves, one behind the other, dousing all of us in the back of the truck with a pale silver gray.

In minutes, Joel aged before our eyes. As if in a time machine, his dark hair bleached white from the dust and his skin, once black as tar, turned a pallid ash. Feet planted, he sat perfectly still, like a stone.

Realizing what was happening, I pulled the bandana off my neck. I had never brought one on a trip before.

*Thank you Lord, I believe you had
something to do with this.*

I had been using them to change the headband on my hat to match my blouses. On especially hot days, I soaked them in cold water and tied them around my neck to keep me cool. Now, passing the black bandana to Jack, I took my pink one, and we each tied them across our noses and mouths, then put on our sunglasses. I giggled thinking we must look like the 'Frito Bandito' gang.

Countless times I yelped when my bottom struck the single board bench below me or my back slammed into the mesh wall behind us, as we vibrated roughly over the rocks.

After six hours of riding the blue bull, we finally turned off the riverbed onto a real road and came to a stop on the side. The quiet alone was overwhelming. I had a headache, my bones creaked, and I was sure I had multiple bruises. We gratefully filed out from the cage. Sticky and gritty. No spit in my mouth, I reached for my Evian bottle for a swig. *I wonder if you make mud pies in your stomach.*

I laughed to Jack, "I'm sure I have a permanent mesh imprint on my back. So would my head, if not for my hat."

"Whew, I'm not believing that ride," he replied.

Tim walked back and forth, rubbing his lower back, "First thing I'm going to do when I get home is visit the chiropractor. I ain't never been slung around that bad in my life."

I looked over at Guard Joel, stepping down from the truck. His face and hair were powdered white. When he removed his round glasses, two big black circles peered back at me. He grinned as I chuckled, then he started smacking the fine, loose sand from his clothes and hair. Time for a quick bush break.

Repositioned in the truck, we drove up a steep incline. Mountain air was cool and fresh. Deep Breath. It felt like it had been forever that I dared to breathe so deeply. We said we were thankful for our jackets. Tall majestic trees seemed to roll by, along with huge full banana trees weighted for the picking.

A large colorful TapTap bus filled with farm workers returning home and villagers going into the city, zoomed past us down the hills. I felt the breeze as they blew by. Several people sat on top with the produce and bags of beans. The bus veered close to the edge of the cliff, then rocked and rolled like a bronco bull at a rodeo trying to dismount its rider. Then another blasted by.

Balek's truck was smoking, as it chugged to a stop on an incline in the middle of the road. Not sure what was happening, one of our guys swung open the metal webbed gate and motioned for us to get out. Which we did.

Shed of its load, the truck sprang to life again, slowly moving forward. As Tim, Jack and I, walked along, following the others behind the truck, we decided among ourselves that the load must have been too heavy straining the motor. We burst out laughing when a man on a donkey passed our truck.

When the road levelled out, we boarded once again.

A few miles later, I awakened from a snooze to shouting. Several of our travelers leaned to our side of the truck, talking rapidly, pointing to the edge of the mountain. Jack and I tried to turn sideways to see what drew their attention. At the bottom of a

steep embankment, a brightly colored Tap Tap bus lay on its side, wheels still spinning. Apparently this happened often, like this picture we took later of a crumpled bus.

Life so vulnerable here, Death so ready to pounce. Twenty-six people died in that crash, we later found out. Not an uncommon event on this mountain. So distressing and sad!!!

The air was more than chilly, as the sun dropped behind the ridge. Only the lights of our three vehicles assured us we were still on the winding path.

Someone yelled, "Not much further."

It's an eerie feeling to arrive somewhere strange, with people you don't know. Darkness all around… Stimulating and exciting, as well as hair-raising.

People as black as the night swarmed us as we pulled into the church grounds, greeting us in their language we knew so little of, and taking our things off the truck, to where, we did not know.

Someone mentioned a bathroom. Flashlights in hand, Tim, Jack and I enthusiastically yet somewhat apprehensively, followed a very large Haitian man, in the blind, up a wooded path.

We arrived at two small rock buildings, much like the outhouse I remember at my grandmother's in Montana. The gentleman unlocked the padlock and laid the latch back, offering his hand in the direction of inside. Lots of trust required to step into that outhouse, knowing this stranger had the power to lock you in, for whatever his reasons might be. A quick prayer Lord.

Protect and Guide us Father that we may know whom to trust and whom to follow.

My small pack of Charmin in hand, I stepped inside. The familiar smell of an outhouse was present, but sweetness of all sweetness, someone had purchased a white toilet seat, complete with lid and had laid it over the single hole. Looking around, I decided the only place for my flashlight was in my mouth. Thankfully it was a small one with a bright light.

When each of us missionaries had taken our leave, the gentle giant locked it all back. Apparently, it was meant for our use alone. This precious man stood by with the key, the entire time we were there, ready and available. Rinsing our hands in a plastic pan, we slung the excess water in the cool mountain air to dry.

We followed the big guy back to a tiny, dimly lit building full of several roughhewn chairs around a long table filled with food. We could finally see the faces of some of our greeters. They had been excitedly anticipating our visit, preparing fruit and chicken with rice for our late arrival. I watched between mouthfuls, as they chattered and hugged our ministry leaders. They seemed happier, this mountain lot. Less tension in their faces and perhaps a little plumper.

They knew we were tired from our trip because through the interpreters, they told Jack and me that we could have the private room, since we were the only married couple there. We called it the *Matrimony Room*. Tim and the rest were taken downhill to sleep on cloth pallets on the floor of the church.

Jack in the Matrimony Room

The Matrimony room was not much larger than one side of the outhouse building. The bed, built with boards nailed together like a knee-high table, not as long as we were, was layered on top by bristly woolen blankets with ragged edges. It was lovely.

I crawled in, dusty and tired. Jack slipped out the door saying, "I have to find some water. My hair feels like a Brillo pad!"

I drifted off to sleep thinking, *these folks have given their best to us... Lord, I am overcome and humbled by their generosity.*

We woke the next morning, Saturday, to the bellowing of a cow. Then, a sudden moan from the same direction. When we stepped out of the Matrimony room, still in our dirty clothes, we met some of the villagers running past. They each nodded, one of them shouting, "Beff." We decided they were explaining the noise, telling us the cow's name.

Standing by the door, a girl in a simple dress, too large for her small body, held a bright orange plastic pan out to me. I don't know how long she had been waiting but she took me by the hand, leading me downhill toward the church. I waved farewell to Jack, then saw him head for the building where we had dinner the night before.

I pointed to myself and said, "Beverly." Then pointed to my little helper.

She replied, "Evelyn." We skipped along the path together.

Strewn nearby over several bushes, lay collared shirts, men's dress pants, faded cotton dresses and skirts, children's clothing and scraps of cloth. Laundry day!

We stopped at a large reservoir of water beside the church. My new friend, Evelyn, mimed for me to scoop the water into the pan she had been holding, then pointed back up the hill.

As I dipped my pan and looked around, it was clear someone had had a rather ingenious idea. Perhaps it was an old idea, but it was new to me. The whitewashed building had a pointed metal roof that hung significantly off one side, but directly over a rock and concrete attached pool. When the rain clouds bumped into the mountains, as they often did, the rain rolled off the roof and collected into the homemade pond, providing much needed water.

In times past, the children spent the day walking down the hills to the river to fill their buckets and returned having sloshed out most of its water. Much like my now half-filled orange plastic pan of water I tried to carry.

Evelyn pushed open a small door beside the Matrimony room. Stooping inside a cave-like space stacked with supplies, I understood I was to freshen up in this dark den. After setting my bath water on some bags of beans and thanking Evelyn, I stepped back inside my room to gather clean clothes and toiletries. Returning to the store room, my eyes adjusted to the dark, and though there was no light to turn on, I saw remarkably well.

Thankful for a quiet girly moment, I stripped off my clothes from the day before, little puffs of dust flying. Swishing my soap and washcloth in the water, I hummed a little tune as I bathed.

"What?" What was that? Did I just hear giggling? Where is that coming from? I wondered.

Hurriedly grabbing for my towel, I banged my head on the ceiling. Combing the place, it dawned on me that the roof line of the building barely grazed the top of the short walls, leaving the tiniest gap. Hence, the reason I could see so well. Blinking back the dark to inspect the ledge, I spotted thirty, maybe forty, little eyes peeking in, one by one, snickering at my birthday suit. I had to laugh, but cried, "Shoo". They scattered, laughing loudly, like only children can do.

Refreshed and ready for the day, I raced over to the kitchen, hoping I had not missed breakfast.

Jack patted the seat next to him. A clear pitcher of coffee with a plate on top sat on the table. Tim and some of the others were also seated around the long table, our leaders at the head. I poured a cup of coffee, listening to talk of the overturned bus we had seen on our way up and this week's upcoming events.

After a plate of scrambled eggs, bread and something that looked like grits, but tasted sweet, I asked our host about the reservoir. The pastor, already dressed in a light-colored suit with a crisp blue shirt and tie, proudly explained, "Several summers ago, the bishop and his wife, brought in a group to put a roof on our church and to build our reservoir, so our children didn't have to walk down the mountain each day."

The Bishop's wife, Madam J spoke up and said, "We have brought another gift for you, Pastor. It is a water tank, *tank dlo,* for the top of your house. The generator we brought will pump water from your reservoir up to the black tub. The force of gravity will then drain water from the tank as needed to various outlets inside your home. We want to help you set that up on our next trip."

There was a round of applause from all of us, for the pastor and his family.

Jack leaned in to me and whispered, "I would love to be part of that." As we dismissed and moved outside, Tim settled into the rocker on the porch to talk with Daniel.

The zesty morning air, along with the panorama of great mountains, invited us for a walk. Jack and I strolled off to enjoy a few moments and to acclimate ourselves to our new surroundings.

As we turned the corner to explore behind some buildings, we nearly fell into an open fire on the ground, hot coals blinking in the mound of ashes. Without warning, I grabbed Jack's arm and shrieked, both of us stopped dead in our tracks. In the center of the coals lay a cow's head. I crinkled my nose, at the smell of burning hair. A small, wiry man, with intense eyes, wearing tan cropped pants and a tattered red t-shirt, squat over the fire, rolling the head in the embers with a thick tree branch. "Beff" he said, as he gave it another prod. We politely smiled and gave our usual nod, then turned back in the direction we had come.

Clear of the building, we broke out in a run, back to the porch, breathlessly talking over each other to Tim and Daniel, "Oh my goodness, you won't believe what we just saw. We heard Beff this morning. "That must be when they slit Beff's throat. "The head, just rolling around…" "And *the* smell…"

Daniel, looking back and forth at each of us, broke out in a grin and declared, "Beff is not the cow's name."

"It's not?" I questioned. "But the villagers… when they ran past this morning…they said "Beff'.

"No," he gently replied, with a sideways smile, "They were telling you, we would have 'beef' for dinner tomorrow. That's a big honor, for the village to kill their only cow for us."

Halted in place, I didn't know what I should say!

Poor Beff, she too gave her all.

Early Sunday morning, I shivered, stepping out from our room. Gathering my jacket and my orange pan, I scurried down the mountain. A misty cloud hung in the air. It soaked the ground, trees and shrubbery, along with a few pieces of yesterday's uncollected laundry.

Pastors, women and children coming from miles away, amassed on the property throughout the day on Saturday, many arriving well into the night. Multitudes now huddled together on cloth pallets in the wet, open air. I felt a sting in my heart for having the Matrimony room.

I spun around to the sound of Tim's voice. "Hey, this place is crawling with people. The church floor has them stacked in there like cord wood. I didn't sleep very much with all the squirming," he said.

"Sorry, Tim. And you're preaching this morning, aren't you?" I asked.

"Oh, that's okay."

Sensing a little irritation, I asked, "You ready to kick off the conference for this week?"

"Sure! I did my studying and preparing yesterday. I'm pretty pumped. Edeline will interpret."

"She's amazing! Works in the office, interprets meetings, oversees all this," I said, as I dipped my pan into the cold water.

"Yeah. You can be praying for her. She told me yesterday, they think she has some kind of a brain tumor or something. She was one of the ministries' orphans, you know. She never mentioned how old she was when they took her in, but, goodness, these kids are exposed to a lot of things; starvation, beatings, dirt and filth. No telling what happened to her. Whatever it is, took its toll on her twenty years."

"Wow, our Edeline. You know Jack and I certainly will pray for her," I turned to leave. Splashing a trail of bathwater, I yelled, "And hey, you're going to do great today,"

The smell of open fires from behind the kitchen and steam rolling from its doors alluded to the grand dinner already cooking. Good memories came to mind of camping trips in the North Carolina and Tennessee Mountains with my son.

After Jack and I dressed for church, we met for breakfast, with our team in the dining hall. A simple meal of cut mangos and bananas, with the usual pitcher of coffee, had been set out and we passed around our granola bars, for those who wanted them. After eating, we prayed together, then Daniel ushered us toward the church.

Working our way to the front through the jam-packed room, we sat in a row of plastic chairs. My eyes took a while to adjust to the semi-darkness. In front of us was a recently built platform. Paolo sat at the keyboard, leading worship, already in full swing. It felt like months since we had been in a service. My heart echoed the song as loud as my voice.

Tim preached a hardy message of encouragement toward trusting God, no matter the circumstances. The pastors who were seated often jumped to their feet, stirred by the power of God's word and Tim's delivery.

Hankies waving in his direction from the heaving crowd fueled his engine even more.

"Keep the faith, even in adversity," he shouted.

As though he had written it himself, he declared I Corinthians 15:58. "Therefore, my dear brothers and sisters, stand firm. Let nothing move you. Always give yourselves fully to the work of the Lord, because you know that your labor in the Lord is not in vain."

Alternating between singing and preaching, the service lasted over four hours. The crowd exited around 1 p.m. Many stopped by to shake hands, as we mumbled a greeting. Eventually, the room emptied.

After the team lingered around the podium, patting Tim on the back and thanking Edeline and the worship group, we stopped to give thanks to the Lord for His presence in the meeting.

Walking outdoors, I was happy to see folks strolling about with plates of food in hand. Many were scouting for a shady spot, the sun now fully exposed. People lined the half-walls and tree stumps, in clusters of ten or more sitting on the ground. A sea of color, like a bowl full of gumballs… Dinner was ready and the mountain air embraced its aroma.

Madam J steered the team, our leaders, and some of the pastors to the small dining hall. Our table had been set with green plates, clear glasses, silverware, and white napkins over hand-made, embroidered tablecloths. Since we were considered the leadership team, we were honored to be included.

But something in me longed to rub elbows with the multitudes down below.

I'm not given to the idea that missionaries in another country are to be lifted up. I had come to serve, was greatly appreciative of all that had been done for us, yet, my discomfort grew.

Michelin displayed her usual flair for food colors. Spread over the table were serving bowls of yellow corn, dishes of diced carrots, plates of sliced tomatoes and mounds of her spicy rice. In the center was a large blue bowl of Beff and gravy. A platter at the other end of the table offered more sliced beef. I knew it was coming, but still felt a twinge for Beff. Neither Jack nor I had eaten beef in over seven or eight years at that point, but we ate a small piece that day. It was tender

The rest of the conference week flowed well. Jack taught pastor workshops, I taught the women leaders. Sometimes, I taught the pastors. Paolo, Edeline, and sometimes Obed, alternated interpreting.

One of my favorite lessons that I taught was on the person of the Holy Spirit, about His role in our lives and how He leads and guides us. I loved teaching them practical ways to cooperate with God, the One who is all Powerful and yet a Gentleman. Then I showed them from God's word how to pray in the Spirit and in the understanding.

My prayer: *Lord, I hold fast to Your promise that my labor for You will accomplish Your purpose and be of value in Your eyes and to Your people.*

Lots of picture-taking with 35mm cameras and my 110 Kodak. Team shots, individual shots, hey-take-my-picture shots, Pastors' and Women's group shots, along with scenery and ordinary daily living…all of us trying to capture this time so we wouldn't forget.

Our week was coming to a close. It blessed me to hear so many say what a refreshing experience it had been for them and how much they learned at the workshops.

Thrilled over the seven people who made a decision to give their life to the Lord, we set up a baptism service on the last day of the conference. Behind the building, where Beff had mooed, was a 10' x 10', five feet deep concrete hole, which the church used to baptize people. No steps, only a handmade rickety ladder.

I was surprised when one of the pastors jumped into the knee-deep, dirty water in his white pants. The first candidate climbed down behind pastor, who at first prayed with him, then dunked him in two feet of water. When he brought him up, these country folk, dressed in their finest, danced around in joy. They thronged together and shouted as if at the pool of Bethesda, where healings took place.

I joined in, excited for the new followers.

Making such a strong commitment in many countries often led to banishment by their family and community. *Thank you Lord, not here.*

The conference ended and I was tired. Jack said he was too, so off we went for what would be our last night in the Matrimony room.

We rose exceptionally early the next day. Going about our morning ritual, I borrowed the bathroom key one last time from the standing sentry.

After locking the door and stepping back into the fresh air, I handed the key to Gentle Giant, who so valiantly cared for us and I thanked him, *Mesi*. He smiled.

Looking around the hillside I did not see anyone anywhere. The masses had dispersed and left for home in the night. I never heard a thing.

Our team assembled at breakfast. Tim said, "Things quieted down pretty good after the exodus, and I slept like a baby."

Our leader announced, "Time to mobilize and return to Carrefour, today. We have a lot of packing to do."

Balek was back in his truck, maneuvering from building to building, rounding up sound equipment, cooking supplies, ministry crates and luggage.

Pastor, his wife and kids, and some of the church members showed up to help. Their generous hearts brought gifts of handmade bowls, cups, hand-painted pictures and special cooked dishes for our journey. A couple of neighbors carried bananas. Not a hand of bananas, but a stalk. It took several guys to lift it overhead and to tie it on top of the truck, where the tank had been. It made me think of the children of Israel bringing grapevines back from the Promised Land.

By noon, we were bursting at the seams again, but ready to roll. We hugged necks, thanking them and assuring them of our return. Like the pioneers that forged their way west, we climbed into place. "Wagons, ho!"

Waving goodbye to the children trailing behind us, something sticking me in my foot stole my attention. Trying to see around my backpack in my lap, I couldn't spot anything. Glowing in the joy of a wonderful week, I settled into the long trip home. I knew we'd reach the riverbed soon. Again, something was sticking me! I tried kicking to break off the stick or to bend the wire, whatever it was.

A rain cloud smacked into us, slowing Balek on the mountain curves. Miles later, we finally stopped on the side of the road for a break. We all filed out. Joel saw me kicking under my seat the whole time. He leaned in to peek underneath where I had been sitting. He grabbed up two live chickens, tied together at the feet. They had been pecking

"Chopsticks" on my ankles, for over an hour. Before resuming, Joel found some twine, tied the clucking hens upside down to the outside of the truck, and left them swinging, like a pair of wind chimes.

We came off the mountain much faster than we went up. Not so many stops. We arrived quickly at the villages near the grasslands, when Bishop J crawled in the back with us, sitting on top of the crates, hunched over. He shared stories about the days his father roamed the mountains on a donkey. His father had established most of the churches in those hills and Bishop J followed in his father's footsteps, caring for the churches and establishing new ones in Haiti.

The sun abandoned the sky, and like before, we followed the car lights ahead. It was still hot without the sun. Suddenly our caravan jarred to a halt! Bishop J nearly fell off the crate, but he quickly said to Tim, Jack and to me, "Cover your heads." The guys in the back attempted to hide Bishop J and us.

Just before I covered, I caught sight of a bonfire in the middle of the street where men and women danced around in a frenzy. I heard voices speaking in harsh tones, then Balek barking back. I sensed Joel's tension, as he listened to the banter, probably wanting to jump out of the truck. But he was too smart to open the cage.

I prayed, and I heard Jack praying under his breath. After a stressed twenty minutes, we began moving along in herky-jerky motion, bumping off the road for a few minutes presumably to drive around the fire.

Sweltering under the tarp, Jack and I came up for air. Bishop J and Tim uncovered as well. All was dark again. The stink from the burning tires lingered, the fire a distant speck.

"What was that all about," Tim asked.

Bishop J said, "That was a voodoo fire. Most of them were in a drunken stupor. They would have taken our cargo and our money… and me, if they had known I was in the truck. I have spoken out publicly against their voodoo practices. They see me as a big threat to them."

We offered up a prayer of thanks to the Lord for keeping us safe, then relaxed back into our seats. I happened to look back at the taillight and discovered our chickens had been plucked from the outside of the truck, the string flapping loose in the wind.

THE ANTEBELLUM

Marilyn, our teammate working at the girls' orphanage, had visited us a few times at the boys' home. She asked if we could hitch a ride to Lamentin for a change. (Lamentin is a small township usually followed by a number. The boys' home was actually Lamentin 55, but was commonly called Carrefour)

Balek, driving the ministry Jeep on Sunday, agreed to take us to see Marilyn after church. I enjoyed smiles and nods with Madam Balek from the backseat, and created a few giggles, making scrunchy faces at their small son and daughter. Jack and Tim rode up front.

As the double metal gate swung open, our motor carriage rolled onto a scene much like that of Gone with the Wind. Not something you would expect to see in the middle of such poverty. Acres of massive pines similar to those in Georgia, coconut palms and mango trees loomed around the grounds, beautifully groomed.

Immediately my heart judged, *"why do our boys live on the concrete jungle...they would love to climb these trees and run, jump, and play."*

Lord forgive me, but it's true, isn't it?

Marilyn strolled onto the porch of the grand white Antebellum, with its manicured flower beds

 surrounding the house. She stood at the top of the stairs with her arms spread wide as well as her great smile. It felt good to reunite with this gracious, uplifting lady.

Balek and his family drove away. The three of us mounted the steps for our embrace and to the open veranda. Stately iron-work overhead connected the two fronts creating a majestic entrance. The entire house meticulously painted white, contrasted with the green, marbled-tile floor.

Marilyn chattered on about her church service, as my eyes took in the massive two story girls' home, an atrium play area at the center. We settled into a circle of chairs to chat.

I felt like little ole' Scarlet O'Hara, expecting any minute for white gloved servants to serve lemonade. As if reading my mind, one of the house mothers appeared with cold glasses of lemonade for each of us. No white gloves!

Out of the corner of my eye, I saw girls peek out from their dorm rooms, like coy southern-belle maidens in colorful, frilly dresses. The brave ones sashayed by us and curled up next to Marilyn. A tiny three-year-old with soulful eyes crawled into my lap, watching my face as I rocked her. She smelled of fresh soap. I noticed her lacy white socks in her pretty black shoes. Each of her many pigtails had colorful barrettes on the ends. We were both content!

Thank you Lord, this one is not out in the traffic with the street babies.

Vita raced round the corner, quite a feat for a woman her size and height. She excitedly said, "I'm so glad you came over today. Welcome to my home."

Vita was the first orphan to arrive at the orphanage twenty-five years before. She now worked for the ministry. Unlike many of the orphans, Vita was a true orphan with no mother or father. She explained that many of the children were turned over to the orphanages by a parent that was unable to feed or clothe them. Mothers often left their baby or child at the mission's gate during the night. The government required the ministry or anyone caring for the children to have a birth certificate for each child present. If the mother did not leave one, the child was removed. Without birth certificates, these children did not exist.

I asked Vita, "Then what happens to them?"

"I don't really know."

No one I asked, while we were there seemed to know exactly where these children were taken. More than likely, put back on the streets.

Vita stood up and pointing toward the rooms said, "Madam Jack, would you like to look around?"

Easing the little one off my lap, I took her by the hand and said to Vita, "Yes, of course.

Would you please ask my little friend if she would like to show me her room?" With a tug and a big grin, she pulled me toward the walkway.

"Mr. Jack, Brother Tim, please wait here on the porch," Vita said, with an apology in her voice, but a smile on her face. "No men are allowed past this point." Both respectfully sat back down.

Marilyn stopped by her small room to drop off her Bible. Hers was the only quarters with a private bath. Water and lights were always available. I never asked how.

We passed the large dining hall where over 200 girls and staff were fed daily. A light breeze blew mercifully through the open doors and windows of the ground floor kitchen beside it.

However, the cooks sweltered, stirring pots, shaped like giant metal bowls, over single burners, spaced along a concrete ledge, some of beans and some of spiced rice… My tummy growled at the aroma. Another house mother stood outside at the long concrete sink that lined the wall, a spigot of running water helping her wash endless plastic plates, cups and other utensils.

As we wandered the halls and peeped in rooms, sweet little girls, draped on their single beds, were brushing each other's hair, playing hand-clapping games, or reading.

The tiny ones were taking an afternoon nap. My tiny one beamed when we stopped in front of her room. After she showed me her cloth dolly with braids like hers, she released my hand and crawled into bed with her for a nap.

"Marilyn," I asked, as we resumed the tour, "where did all these lovely dresses I see hanging in each room come from? There's so many, I am pleasantly surprised."

"I asked the same question, not long after I got here." Marilyn shared. "One of the girls in the office said a large ministry had visited the orphanage and shipped a truckload of different size dresses. And, of course, some of the girls' sponsors send dresses, too."

"I, myself," she continued, "brought a suitcase full of socks and underwear for the girls. The market in Port O Prince has some good buys on that stuff, so every time I go, I buy more."

Marilyn and I returned to Jack and Tim. Then she led us across the 'plantation' to the Doctors' Quarters, an acre away.

As we passed the monstrous skull of an unfinished building, Tim said, "That was supposed to be a hospital. There was some kind of falling out with the people involved and it was never completed."

Jack thumbed me to look behind us. A guard stealthily trailed us, with a rifle slung over his shoulder, not something you typically see around a ministry. I caught a glimpse of him walking the grounds earlier but still fought off a shiver.

Marilyn led us into a luscious contemporary two-story home, where our lunch was set up in an air conditioned dining room, next to an also air conditioned, recently built kitchen. I was embarrassed in front of Michelin, but she and her two helpers, smiled sweetly at us from behind the shiny tiled countertop.

Little did we know there was a shadow hanging over this place that would soon stun us all.

Me carrying laundry Haitian style

DOCTORS' QUARTERS

After a delicious dinner at the Doctors' Quarters, Marilyn stood up, and excitedly said, "Ready to stretch your legs? Come on I'll show you the place."

During dinner, we had had a vigorous discussion about the business of the unopened hospital. Well, Marilyn and Tim had a lot to say. Details were interesting, and I knew some of the people involved, but Jack and I mostly listened, not offering opinions.

Doctors' Quarters was intended for physicians who would one day visit from the U.S. to help in the hospital. It was designed to be a comfortable relief for them at the end of a hot day, but looked more like a mansion on a canal in West Palm Beach.

Palms swayed outside, like they were giant paint brushes coloring the exterior walls a tropical flamingo pink, set-off beautifully by the white-on-white tile on the floor that trailed up the stairwell. Large archways trimmed in white, framed entrances and windows. Terra cotta tiles capped the massive roof. Extremely striking contrast to the sights outside the gate.

After a filling meal, we finally rose from the table, ready to walk off some of our dinner. Looking around from dining room to kitchen, I saw the latest in appliances, including an ice maker, dishwasher, microwave, and industrial size refrigerator and stove. Michelin was humming at the sink as she washed our dishes by hand.

Marilyn laughingly lamented, "Lord, lord, you should have seen this place. The cleaning girls were scrubbing all this shiny tile with harsh chemicals intended for mason walls. I had to teach them not to scrub the finish off. Look here, the counter tops already have a few dull places.

I shot a glance toward the sink, wondering if Michelin understood what we were talking about.

Marilyn kept shaking her head, leading us from the kitchen to the outside breezeway that ran through the center of the house. The white floor tile trailed up a wide cascade of welcoming stairs.

Private rooms with baths lined the hallway on the left. Behind the kitchen and to the right, was a laundry room, complete with electric washer and gas dryer. Marilyn had suggested we bring our clothes to wash, while we were here.

For weeks our things had been hand-washed in plastic bowls and line dried, by the cleaning ladies. Our clothes were scratchy and towels exfoliating, however, our whites were brilliant and unblemished.

In back of the laundry room were two small rooms for on-site security people. We shook hands with them, Jean and Tomas. They were paid a small wage to protect the lodge.

As we climbed the steps to the second floor, we stopped on the landing to take in the beautiful view of the grassy lawn.

The next level had a common area decorated with leather couches and furniture placed conversationally. A small television sat on a table at one end. Rows of more private rooms and baths extended to the left.

But the true beauty was the fabulous sight from the balcony. My eyes charted a path through the palms to a view of the ocean's smooth, aqua blue. My soul savored the seascape.

Since we had no classes to teach until Wednesday, Tim, Jack and I decided to stay a couple of days. All of us, including Marilyn *camped out* in the Quarters. Marilyn and I occasionally strolled up hill to the Antebellum to visit the girls.

Once again, I was jolted by the sight of the guard with his gun, staying nearby and alert. It wasn't clear until much later why he was needed.

Rising before daybreak, I retrieved coffee from the kitchen and eased quietly to the balcony. Hugging my Bible close to heart, I caught a sunrise kiss from my Lord. Basking in His presence, I lay back in the lounge and listened for His heartbeat.

Teach me your ways, my precious Lord. For your ways are higher than mine. Be still and know that I am God, I hear you say. I choose to be still, Lord. Here am I.

We prayed individually. As a husband and wife, Jack and I have often enjoyed special times of prayer. And there is great power in unity.

In a hub of sensitivities before God, our team prayed fervent prayers together those few days, read passages of scripture from God's word, and stirred ourselves up like David and his men in Ziklag.

Yes, washing laundry, but also washing our souls with the washing of the water of the Word. As iron sharpens iron, so one person sharpens another, says Proverbs 27:17

God prepared our hearts for what lie ahead. *Thank you, all knowing Lord.*

EASTER

Easter was coming and we wanted to do something special for our boys. We knew the girls would have their frilly dresses, so we decided to buy each of the boys an outfit for Sunday church service. Magdalena, wife of the Haiti VBI director, who often helped with the boys' home, made an itemized list of names with shirt and pant sizes.

Armed with our list, we called for Vita, once again, to take us to market. She arrived at the base with Balek in the white Jeep. Balek said he had business in town and could take us to the market, but we would have to ride back by TapTap. Daniel came with us.

Once we were dropped off, Vita and Daniel led us deep into the market. Jack nodded to people along the way, and I excitedly skipped along, smiling, happy to be among them.

Suddenly, a snarling vendor pointed at us and called out, "Chin, Chin." Daniel scooted us past him.

Vita's back straightened, her eyes darting all around, like a mother hen ready to protect her chicks. For a moment, I thought she was going to wrap us in her long skirt. We heard those words muttered several times, as Daniel and Vita walked us quickly towards the center stalls of children's clothing.

Confused, I stopped Daniel and asked, "What are they saying. Did we do something wrong?"

He pulled us aside and said, "They believe anyone who is fairer skinned than they are, is Chinese, (Chin). I heard one saying you have the SARS virus and they are afraid."

At the airport, Jack and I had been stopped for a screening of the SARS virus, before arriving in Haiti. People wearing surgical masks sat at long foldout tables. With clipboards in hand, they asked a few questions, then directed us to pass under a metal archway that checked our temperature.

The story we heard, possibly rumor, was that President Clinton had offered a substantial amount of money to assist countries infected by the SARS virus, in particular China. This prompted Haiti's president to find a way to cash in on Clinton's funding. Therefore, he somehow gave special invitation to the *Chin* to come to Haiti.

The possibilities of the SARS virus swept the country into a panic.

Due to the unrest, we decided to finish our shopping quickly. I knew Daniel needed to leave, which meant Vita would have to take us home alone. But the bargaining between stalls took longer than we planned. Finally thrilled with our purchases, we divided the pants and the cute pastel shirt and tie sets into three large plastic mesh bags. Each of us carried one, except Daniel who bid us farewell and left.

Outside the market area, we talked Vita into letting us pick up a couple of items for our supporters. Reluctantly, she took us to a row of sidewalk merchants near the Palace. We bought several postcards of Haiti and hand-painted refrigerator magnets of local scenes from town, then followed Vita to the corner to look for Tap Tap.

The Tap Tap we caught was a painted school bus, like we saw on the mountain trip, with passengers lying on the rooftop. Vita hustled us and our packages inside an already full bus. The small seats held three or four persons to a seat.

Vita chose her place and thrust two folks over with her hefty hips and bag. We had to split up, so I slid onto a seat nearby, securing my package between my feet. Jack, always the gentleman, returned to the front looking for a place to land and finally inched next to two older ladies and a child.

The bus chugged forward. Between the frequent stops for the Tap Tap's new fares, I balanced one cheek on and one cheek off the bus seat. Though overly crowded, somehow room was made for the proverbial, "one more".

The traffic thinned out, allowing the bus driver some running room. As he gained speed, a sudden jarring toppled a man off the roof and onto the road. When I gasped, many passengers looked back, but otherwise, showed little disturbance. The bus did not stop. Cringing back into my seat, I called out, "Jack," searching for his face and clutching my chest. He was too far away to hear over the noise of the bus and I couldn't catch his eye. I wept, praying…

Lord, we just drove off and left a human being hurt on the road. I don't understand, but Lord, please send someone to help him. I pray healing for his body and life over him.

I gripped myself until we stepped off the bus a block from the base, where I choked on my words, as I relayed to Jack and Vita what I saw. With a swish of her hand, as if brushing away a moth, Vita said, "Oh yeah, it happens all the time."

"Vita," I pleaded, "I can't believe the bus didn't stop to see about the guy. Will someone care for him?"

"I don't know," she shrugged. "Most people don't want to get involved." Sounded like the story in the Bible about the Good Samaritan, when the others passed by the beaten man.

My Jack and I clung to our bags and each other, as we walked the muddy road back to the base. Muttering to each other, we realized there was nothing we could do. We won't even know until heaven what happened to that poor man.

Swallowing our sorrow, we put on a happy face to deliver our gifts to the boys.

It was an ordered chaos, as Magdalena attempted to check the list. Our guys exuberantly grabbed for their favorite colored shirt, tossing packages overhead to one another. Peals of laughter in between... Several slipped in and out from the table, holding pants up to their waists. I hoped they all had what they would need for the next morning.

Easter Sunday in Haiti! I wondered what my family was doing in the States.

My favorite holiday, because of the Resurrection. Easter promises life and newness, darkness lifting. Spring dressed in fresh air and vibrant flowers wearing white shoes. It meant starting over, like my husband proposing to me one Easter Sunday afternoon.

He and I walked hand in hand reminiscing on the way to church, then found our seats at the front.

Light of the World was on the program to sing and Jack would play the drums.

After the music started, our handsome boys, hair slicked in place, purposefully strutted across the front of the church, as if on parade.

Big grins and little waves, a few high fives with Jack… They sat tall on the benches facing out from the right side of the room, reminding me of a basket full of lively pastel-colored eggs.

I felt so proud for them in their new clothes. No Easter outfit I ever wore felt this good.

The boys in their new Easter clothes.

THE OASIS

I've always loved that my birthday was in April and on the 27th. It's a unique date, not many people share. But when Jack and I married in May on the seventh, it allowed me to celebrate not only my birthday, but our anniversary and then a week later Mothers' Day. Almost a month of celebration and this year all the festivities would be in Haiti.

We had been in Haiti long enough that Jack was in need of a haircut. Obed offered to take him to a local barber, but when it came time, Jack backed out, saying to me, "Can't you just trim my hair?"

"I can, but you know that's not my expertise. I cut my own bangs sometimes. But the only scissors I have with me are cuticle scissors."

"That'll work."

"Well, you know, cuticle scissors have a curve, right?" I said. But he insisted.

Sitting Jack on a stool and placing a towel around his shoulders, I, nervously took the cuticle scissors and snipped away. I thought I did pretty well, until I stepped back to take a look. There were little patches of curved hair sections all over his head. The bottom edge in the back was scalloped. *Oh, dear!* Jack never fussed at me.

Carrefour, Haiti had its routine difficulties. Cold shower dribbles and razor burns. Bug bites and interrupted sleep. Now add bad haircuts along with no power! We figured a little time out for celebration would be nice.

So when Daniel arrived early before *Light of the World* came that day, we took a moment to ask him, "What does one do to celebrate a special time like an anniversary, Daniel? Where could we go?"

Ever resourceful, Daniel answered, "I know just the place. Let me make a phone call for you."

He was rapidly talking and I felt my eyebrows following his facial expressions, when he closed his phone and announced, "I have a reservation for a motel for you, tomorrow. It is near Port au Prince."

Our singers gathered on the porch, as we thanked Daniel.

After a night of voice and instrument practice, Light of the World broke into singing the happy birthday song for me. Misty tears collected in the corners of my eyes, and rolled down my face. My heart melted like a chocolate bar left on a sunny window sill, as they took turns sharing their congratulations! I embraced each one of them and thanked them for a lovely birthday.

The next morning, as Jack and I packed an overnight bag, I threw in the book my friend Lisa handed me as I boarded the plane for Haiti. She knew I loved to read, and said "This is a story about Haiti I thought you might enjoy."

The book was called, *Twenty Cents for an Angel*, by Hector Charles. During the flight, I enthusiastically waved the partially read book in the air and said to Jack, "I would love to meet this man. Wouldn't it be funny if we ran into Hector in Haiti?" Impossible!

Finally packed, we scrambled for the door as a blasting horn signaled our driver's arrival at the base. We hugged Tim a hasty goodbye.

Another breakneck ride, buffeted left and right. Staring out the window, I noticed a long Viaduct meant to route flood waters off the land. Jack pulled out the camera and started taking pictures out the window again. Instead of a clear path for emergency run-off, the channel was filled instead with garbage, empty bottles, cartons, carcasses and every kind of stink.

I wondered, "There must not be a system in place for garbage trucks to haul this stuff away."

Jack commented, "That would be a good business for someone to start. There's certainly a need for it."

"Trouble is, it would probably rot in the trucks with this heat, stuck in the web of traffic on Haiti Hwy 95," I said.

Balek's truck ground to a halt before a large unpainted metal gate. Once again, embarrassingly laid on the horn until someone peeped out through a small opening. A few words of Creole to the gatekeeper, and Balek motioned for us to grab our things.

We pulled our small bags from the cab and adjusted them across our shoulders. Before we reached the door, Balek was gone.

I found myself grinning at the possibilities. Was it a dump? Did they indeed have running water and good food? What lay behind these walls?

Lush green palms, tropical plants and manicured flower beds of purples, yellows, and reds surrounded adorable small cabins. Paved walkways wandered off to the pool. Clean, fresh! My lungs breathed easy to the fragrance of the flowers. True to its name, it was an Oasis!

Turning on the lights, hubby and I danced around our air conditioned, dustless room. We nearly shouted in excitement when we turned the knob on the bathroom sink and it instantly spewed out hot water. We luxuriated in the smallest things.

Lunch was delicious, served on white linen. *Wouldn't Michelin, our cook, love to work here, Lord.*

We changed our clothes and bumped shoulders, laughing together as we ambled down the colorful path to the pool. Spreading our spotless white towels over chaise lounges, we welcomed the balmy Caribbean breeze.

A loud-talking, white-haired gentleman with multiple rings on his fingers sauntered up and stood in front of us, blocking the sun. After exchanging names, our new acquaintance, Ken said with a deep southern drawl, "Are you guys Americans? What brings you to Haiti?"

We explained to him about our Bible school internship in Carrefour, which, by his nods and comments, indicated he found it interesting. We in turn asked, "So what brings you here?"

"Oh," he replied, "my wife and I do Bible Studies at the motel. This week we have a guest speaker with us. That's him sitting over there under the umbrellas."

"Yeah, I noticed him earlier and the people with him. What does he teach?

"He teaches local pastors, specializing in the subject of dealing with voodoo in Haiti."

"Really," Jack piped in, "What's his name?"

"Hector Charles. Why don't you guys join us for dinner and I'll introduce you."

Back in our room, I savored the hot shower but didn't linger. Nervous with excitement, I slipped on my sundress and shawl, then a matching necklace and bracelet Jack had given me. I took his arm for our walk to dinner.

Ken introduced us. Hector Charles was a lovely man, his poster slightly bent in his light colored shirt, navy slacks and matching jacket. There were hints of gray in his dark hair. He spoke English well, just a trace of a Creole accent.

As I shook his hand, I said, "Tonight we celebrate my birthday and our anniversary. You are not here by coincidence, Mr. Hector, but by divine invitation. As are we."

His gentle eyes smiled back at me as he patted my hand. "How is that, Mrs. Jack?"

I told him about Lisa's gift and shared my remark of my hope to meet him. "God has always given me little presents on my birthday and at Christmas. I believe you are a gift to us tonight."

Indeed, a delightful gift.

Our dinner companions refreshed the ice in our glasses, adding more soda. Jack and I hummed quietly, arm in arm, as we left the dining room and followed the little lights outlining the happy trails. We all returned to the chairs around the tables at the poolside cabana.

Jack, not having read the book, asked Hector, "Why did you name your book, *Twenty Cents for an Angel?*"

Hector swallowed, setting his cola aside and began his story. "I once walked along a dry river bed going to the next village to preach. I didn't realize that the river was washing swiftly down from the mountain.

Suddenly, the river filled with rapidly moving water, scooping my feet from under me. Tumbling over and over, the swirls held me beneath the crashing waves. Panic took over, since I did not know how to swim. I whispered a prayer but still no air. After what seemed an eternity, I heard someone call out, 'Mr., hello.'"

"I bobbed up to see a large black man on the edge of the bank. I sputtered."

"Just when I plummeted down again, I felt the man's two strong arms reach across my chest and pull me to himself, dragging me to the side."

"Breathing rapidly, I stood to my feet and quickly thought, 'I want to give this man something for saving my life.' As I fished for the twenty cents in my pocket, I looked up to find the man was gone. I turned my face to the sky, nothing. Nothing downstream, no bush to hide behind, no house nearby. Gone! 'Twenty cents for an angel,'" he concluded.

I felt like a small girl, clapping for joy at a favorite story told by her Father. I wanted to jump to my feet, applauding, instead I sat grinning and offered up a quiet "Amen."

We spent an enchanted evening with Hector as story after story from his book came alive.

Oh, Lord! You are a good good Father to me. Thank you for the life of Hector Charles.

Thank you so much for my birthday present.

BOYS, BEACH, AND BEBE

My love for the boys grew deeper each day. Many times I reached for these little guys offering Momma hugs. Some accepted with open arms, some, like Bebe, stood like a statue.

Bebe had a melon shaped head with close cropped hair. His big dark eyes gave him a wounded puppy look, somber and silent. I often centered on hugging Bebe, sensing he seemed to need it the most.

He never refused but he didn't hug back. I looked for ways to enjoy life with him and the other boys.

I surprised them, one afternoon, by joining their soccer game on a concrete court. My long skirt flying and flip flops dashing about, the game soon changed to keep-away-from-Beverly. They thrust out their chests and grinned with an eyeful dare to come take the ball.

Little James teased the ball back and forth in front of me, then snatched it away, scooting behind me. He gasped inward, shocked, when my long legs slipped a foot in, and with ball in tow, headed for the goalie. Short lived glory, they were too fast and nimble and the ball was soon missing from between my feet.

We laughed and scrambled for hours, stopping only for a quick draw from our water bottles. Some of the house mothers nearby giggled, shaking their heads at me. The sun set on us, as our neighbors peered from the gate, watching the white woman play boy games. Jack got a kick out of the whole scene.

The Antebellum girls had their lovely acres to play on, but my heart wanted to do something to take our lads away from the concrete dwelling. Surrounded by some of the most beautiful shorelines in the world, and my favorite pastime, I talked with Jack and Tim about a beach picnic.

We spoke with our leaders and they agreed to the trip, as long as we were willing to fund it with our own money, including gas for the truck. Our boys were so often overlooked, we decided to do whatever was necessary to make this excursion happen.

Even Michelin played a part. She prepared their favorite meal: chicken with beans and rice. She filled the pots we had taken on the mountain trip. The dull-silver pots stacked one on top of the other (five in all) topped with a lid. It was shaped much like the leaning tower of Pizza, without the lean. We iced down cases of fruit-flavored Tampico drinks and packed several bags of cookies. Beach time…

I smelled the excitement in the air, as our guys circled and clambered onto the back of Balek's truck. Typical children, they poked and jabbed as they jockeyed for their places on the benches. A couple of older boys called "dibs" on the front seat.

We arrived at a gated opening with a large sign that read "private beach," and a price. More expense we weren't aware of. The ministry was adamant, we would be safer here. When someone finally came to the gate, he proceeded to count heads. The cost was per person. We dug around for all the gourdes we had.

Lord, we can't turn back now.
We need Your help.

Balek shifted on his feet, then speaking through one of the older boys, Balek said he had some money we could borrow. Happily, all twenty-seven of us made it in.

Thank You, Lord.

Our precious boys didn't jump out of the parked truck and run off. Instead, each grabbed supplies from the back, took them to a small pavilion and set up the picnic tables. Sunshine was high with warm gentle breezes. It set the stage for a gorgeous Tuesday.

Ripping their shirts off, the gang headed for the water. It never occurred to me they didn't have swim suits. They dove in with whatever else they had on. Neither did it occur to me till that moment, I was the only female on the outing.

The guys were already swimming, splashing and dunking each other by the time I climbed down the rocks lining the shore. Easing into the water, I noticed Bebe sitting off to the side, eyes wide and breathing quick. When I inched next to him, I said softly, "Come on Bebe, the water feels good."

He looked out at the other boys, then swung his head side to side so hard that his cheeks jiggled. He was twelve, going on thirteen, and I thought his manhood among the older boys would be in question if he didn't get in the water soon. Fear in those eyes begged me not to let them see.

He knew a little English, so I spoke comforting words to him. I discreetly, reached out my hand calling, "Come on, Bebe, I got you. It's okay, I got you."

Bebe slid slowly off the rock, trembling so hard he made ripples in the water. He latched onto my outstretched arm like a baby bird to a limb after his first flight. I thought he might fight and struggle but he just clung to me with all he had. Feet kicking underneath, they finally touched bottom. He stood blinking, looking me in the eye. I bobbed up and down. He copied.

One of the boys yelled, "Hey Bebe, catch." I figured that's what he said because his arm was cocked back with a ball in hand. Gripping me, Bebe slung his right arm out to catch the ball. No one noticed his other hand, as he returned the throw, they continued playing catch.

Before long, Bebe's face relaxed, as he splashed around with the other guys in chest-high water, enjoying his victory over the sea.

Later when we stopped to give thanks over our picnic, Bebe slipped me a mango Tampico - my favorite. The boys filled up on their dinner and handfuls of cookies. Some tossed a Frisbee in the sand, some read, most returned to swim.

Jack took lots of pictures.

At day's end, we surprised the boys with a bag of Tootsie Pops from Tim's private stash. We all flopped around in the truck bed, salty from the ocean, but smiling with white sticks hanging out our mouths.

Home at last, tired from our romp in the sun, we unloaded our gear between hugs and thanks. Bebe bee-lined straight for me and gave me a lingering hug.

Thank you Lord, You said love never fails. I know this pleased You. This was a huge highlight for me on this trip.

THE DREAM

Morning came like any other for Tim, Jack and me.

Michelin had prepared a colorful but lightweight breakfast. That was fine with me, since I woke feeling uneasy. I had had a serious dream the night before. I kept it to myself, but it was tethered to my mind, like a balloon tied to my foot.

Tim passed the toast to Jack and said, "I think I'm going to change rooms to the one up front."

Not wanting to come across spooky spiritual, I slowly said, "Well Tim, I feel like I need to tell you something. I had a weird dream last night." He nodded and then I had both their attentions.

"I don't want to scare you, but I dreamed you were lying on your bed, right in front of the window like you have it now, and someone stuck a long-nose gun through the jalousie and shot you."99

"That's it," he said, "I know I'm moving now. I believe the Lord is warning us," Tim said.

A few nights later, Jack and I woke to the sound of gun shots going off up in the hills behind us. Suddenly, there was a rattling at the door of the house. We quietly eased the solid dresser in front of our room door, praying for protection and for Tim, now at the end of the hall.

After some time passed, we slid the dresser back and stuck our heads out the door and saw Tim. He asked, "Did ya'll hear them gun shots?"

"Yeah," Jack said, "what's going on?"

Tim continued, "I don't know, but when I heard someone coming in the house, I called out to ya'll, but I guess you didn't hear me. I waited a while and finally decided, well if I get shot, I'll be with Jesus. I stepped out into the hall and ran into Beatrice. She had come over to check on us."

"Oh, thank you Lord, I'm so glad we're all okay. I believe the Lord was keeping us safe, again," I said.

***

Ezra, orphaned as a child, now a young man in his twenties, dropped in on us when we first arrived in Carrefour. He loved the Lord, and had heard missionaries were staying at the boys' home. Because he enjoyed asking questions about the Bible and speaking in English, he often stopped by after work. He was a tailor.

One day, we popped in on him at his job. The shop housed six black, very old model Singer sewing machines, placed randomly around the mini-factory, the size of a large walk-in closet. Shirts, dresses, and clothing at various stages of completion hung around the room.

Madam J had insisted I have a dress made as a souvenir of my visit to Haiti. *I suspected she felt bad for me in the drab clothes I had brought.* She drove me to town to buy material in what looked like a cluttered Fabrics "R" Us store, bolts of cloth from floor to ceiling, wall to wall. I bought a couple of yards of an inexpensive, brightly-colored flower print.

I now held it out before Ezra, and described the style dress I was looking for. He gave me a really good price, and said he would let me know when it was ready. Three days later, I had a lovely new outfit for Sunday that fit amazingly well.

When Jack and I returned from our trip to the tailor shop, we found Daniel and Tim once again with their heads together. We had seen this many times since the mountain trip. Tim finally told us he wanted to help Daniel and his soon to be wife, Maribel to start an orphanage.

Daniel had brought over Laura9999999, a little girl who had only a short stump of a left arm. Dressed in a pretty, pale orange dress, she waved with her only hand from a chair near the door. Her eyes were bright and like Nemo, didn't seem self-conscious of her arm.

Daniel said, "Her mother can no longer care for her. If we don't help her, she will probably end up on the streets. Because of her disfigurement, she would likely be abused. These are the kind of children Maribel and I want to care for in our home."

Daniel asked, "Can you guys follow me up the hill from here? I have something I want to show you." We agreed. Esther left with Beatrice and I went to put my dress away.

We followed Daniel out a back entrance to the compound. Not having ventured in that direction before, I was struck by the massive mountains that hugged our borders.

After an exhausting hike over rough rocks and steep steps, we arrived, grimy and sweaty, in front of a narrow stone house with an open doorway. Daniel called out in Creole, as we stooped inside. It took a moment to pull into focus the surroundings.

There on a makeshift bed sat two children. The boy was the oldest, maybe six or seven, and the little girl was about three years old.

Before we left the base, I had shoved a handful of candy and a couple of small toys in my pocket. As Daniel told us their story, I held out a matchbox car to the boy and a tiny pink slinky to the girl. Her hair was tangled and her eyes were noticeably crossed. It took a couple of tries for her to grasp the little wire toy. "Their mother and father died. I'm not sure how. The neighbors tell different stories. John and Sophie have no family and live alone. The people next to them, their houses share a common wall, throw food over to John and Sophie every once in a while. They say they can't afford to feed them every day and don't want the responsibility."

"No one cares for them, they are alone here, day and night?" I whispered, emptying my pockets of candy onto the bed. Tears pricked the backs of my eyes, but I swallowed them down.

Daniel nodded, "Yeah."

"And school? Isn't the boy old enough to be in school?" asked Jack.

"Without help, that's not going to happen for him. He needs uniforms, supplies, shoes, not to mention supervision."

He turned toward the little girl, "Sophie needs medical attention for her eyes soon, before she is too old to have corrective surgery. "

"Wow, what kind of help is available here in Haiti?"

"As I said, no one here wants to get involved and many of them cannot. There's no government assistance available for children in this situation. That's why I want to start an orphanage, to at least give these children the opportunity I had as an orphan." He shifted on his feet, as if waiting for an answer.

Lord, what can we do, we have so little, they need so much. You love the children, Lord.

What would you have us to do?

We played with the children for a while. Then stepped outside to have Daniel take our picture with big brother and little sister, sitting on a boulder near the house. I glanced over next door, and to my surprise, I saw a small television set playing. Lounged in front were a couple of adults and several small children. *Where are they getting the electricity from, how on earth did they afford this luxury, what shows would there be in Creole, I wonder?*

Anticipating my question, Daniel tilted his head toward them and replied, "Probably pimps out either the wife, or a child, like the street babies we saw." The family barely had clothes or anything else.

I shook my head, as if trying to escape the thought that this was a regular occurrence among the poor in Haiti. "We will pray, Daniel, to see what we can do to help. Thank you for bringing us."

We had finally spread our wings and flown the coop, leaving the base more often than we did in the beginning.

The next day, Daniel asked Tim to go look at a house he heard was available. We asked to go along. The VBI-Haiti director offered to take us in his car. It was an old model Fiat, dented and worn, inside and out. The sunlight sparkled on the cracks of the windshield making mini rainbows, distorting the view.

I wondered if we may have been better off walking as we choked on the dust swirling in through the open windows, not able to close them for the intense heat. Not to mention, five adults crammed inside. I tugged at my blouse sticking to my skin, flapping the ends for a small breeze.

We pulled up to the empty row house, if it could speak, it would beg for attention. But with lots of rooms, a decent kitchen and a small yard, it had great potential. An iron gate extended across the carport for security. In order to rent a house in Haiti, you had to pay a year's lease, in advance. This would be the first hurdle.

Tim and Daniel negotiated and planned for the next several days. Tim spent hours at the smelly Cyber Café down the street, emailing supporters back home about Daniel's idea.

John and Sophie would be their first two children at the orphanage. Jack and I gave our personal money for John to return to school, and for Sophie to receive the treatment needed for her eyes. We promised to send more when we returned home and resumed working.

Daniel jumped and danced circles around our living room at the thought of realizing his dream for a home.

DEATH AND DEPARTURE

The squatty phone alarmingly burst to life on its perch one morning. It seldom rang. I rarely answered because I couldn't get past, "Bon Jour, sorry no Creole." Tim grabbed the receiver, as Jack and I padded down the hall from our room toward him. We leaned in to listen. Within seconds, Tim's face went grim.

"What is it Tim?" I asked.

He didn't answer but continued with the caller, "Okay, we'll be there as quick as we can. We'll be praying."

He faced us and said, "Marilyn has just been through a terrible nightmare. She went down to the Doctors' Quarters to do laundry this morning…" He hesitated. "She…she found Jean and Tomas dead in the breezeway…Blood everywhere."

"Oh no, the security guys?" Jack exclaimed. He shook his head. "Is Marilyn alright, what happened?"

"Yeah, she's pretty shook up. Even as a nurse, she said she'd never seen anything like this."

I blurted out, "Well, let's go get her and bring her back here, don't you think?"

We all agreed, then Jack took a moment to lead us in prayer.

Tim tried to call for a ride but now couldn't get a dial tone. We each fiddled around, stuffing a few things in our backpacks. Jack paced the floor. I read the same Bible verse several times, as I sat speechless at the table. The minute hand on my watch flew by like seconds.

Tim kept poking at the phone. We were prepared to walk the two miles, if necessary, but knew that wasn't the safest plan. Another hour went by.

Daniel suddenly walked into our living room. Before he could speak, Tim cried, "Hey Daniel, did you hear what happened at Lamentin?"

"Yeah I did, that's why I came over."

"We need to be with Marilyn. Can you get us a ride?"

"Yeah, sure," he said. Daniel snapped open his cell phone and tried to reach one of the leaders in the ministry. No connection, nothing! He was about to take us outside the base to catch a Tap Tap, when we heard the familiar sound of the truck squeal to a stop at the gate.

Joel apparently already left for Lamentin. Another man I'd never seen before opened the gate for Balek.

After a brief interchange, Daniel turned to us and said. "Balek told me it's pretty bad over there. They can't figure out how the killers got in, but Balek says Jean and Tomas were brutally attacked, their tongues savagely cut out."

The air was hot and stuffy but the hairs on my arm stood up and I shivered.

Oh, Lord! I don't believe what I am hearing. Please protect Marilyn. This is awful. Help us, Lord, to know what to do. How to walk this out. We need You!

We need Your protection, Your peace and Your wisdom.

The wall totally surrounded the Antebellum! How did they climb over that huge wall with the cut glass on top? And where was the armed guard? Were Marilyn and the girls okay? My heart prayed as my mind raced, searching for answers. But most importantly, I wanted my eyes on Marilyn.

Normally, my husband didn't like Balek's driving, but at that moment, I suspected Jack didn't really care how fast he drove.

After we arrived at Lamentin, the gate guard hesitantly opened one side, refusing to let us enter, until Balek jumped out and explained why we were there.

Bounding from the truck, I found Marilyn sitting on the veranda, knitting her fingers in her lap. She rose from her seat as I raced up the stairs, nearly knocking her over with a hug. Grabbing her by the shoulders, I then stepped back to take her in. Satisfied Marilyn was safe and untouched, I held her close. Jack and Tim gathered around to give her a hug, each whispering comforting words.

Tension was high, as if an electrical cable had broken loose, snapping in the air. Not having experienced much death in my life, the magnitude of such cruelty was pricking my whole body. Such a vile, inhuman act seemed to leave its mark on all of us.

At Marilyn's request, Tim, Jack and I walked with her to the Quarters to look around. She pointed at the walls, the floor and up the stairs, talking loud and fast, "Covered in blood… everything…in all my years of nursing, I never saw bodies so mutilated," she said, tears finally flowing.

"Oh Marilyn, I can't imagine what that was like," I said, feeling my words fall like empty bags to the floor.

Fumbling with her thoughts, Marilyn eventually poured out the details of the gory scene. "I had to go back to the Doctors' Quarters to clean up the mess. I couldn't leave it like that. Jean and Tomas' parts removed. Oh my Lord, they were cut and chopped… I tried to get the housekeepers to go with me, but they were too scared to go." She took a breath.

"Oh my Lord, Marilyn, you went by yourself?" I said, barely believing what I was hearing.

"Yeah! On the way, I snagged a guy that keeps the grounds to follow me down there to help me move their bodies…and all. We, we…lugged them into the laundry room and I found a blanket to cover them up."

"Marilyn, where were the guys with the guns we always saw walking around here?" Jack asked.

"They normally stay close to the girls' home at night."

"Didn't they see or hear anything?" Tim implored.

"Yeah, I don't know…apparently they were either sleeping or in on it," she said.

It seemed that no CSI crew was coming to the crime scene. After Marilyn's super cleanup job, only a pale evidence of blood now clung to the grouted edges of the tile. There was not much left for us to do.

Crooking my arm in Marilyn's, we stumbled back to the Antebellum, not having opened the door where Jean and Tomas lay.

The older girls had left for school while the little girls hid, tucked away in their rooms. The assisting mothers watched over them. Occasionally, a head popped out a doorway, but like tiny turtles, quickly slipped back inside the room.

I shadowed Marilyn to her chambers to help her pack a few things.

Loading ourselves back into the truck, we stole Marilyn away, distancing her from the danger. We brought her back to our house.

The guys set her things in the room next to Tim's, across the hall from Jack and me. One by one, we re-assembled on the porch.

"You realize that God kept us," I said, feeling the magnitude fall in my lap.

"I remember, we had talked about staying at the Quarters overnight," Jack added, lifting his hands in thankfulness. "Thank you, Lord!"

"Yeah, that's right, we were undecided whether to go this week or maybe the next," said Tim. "Glory to God, last minute we decided...not to go."

Each of us, nodded and prayed aloud, prayers of thanksgiving.

You preserved us, Lord. Thank You for protecting Marilyn and all of us.

Oh, Lord, those two young men...

Talking seemed to soothe Marilyn, but didn't appease her questions. "Who are these killers? How could they possibly have gotten inside? Why did they come?" she rattled on.

We alternated between sitting quietly and rehashing events for hours, not finding any answers.

Beatrice, Paolo's sister, called us to dinner. She had stepped in to cook for us, since Michelin was needed at the Antebellum.

The next couple days, we stayed inside the house, close together. Each one of us talked about how our attention was heightened, especially at night. Then word came by way of Paolo for us to return to Lamentin.

Upon arriving, we found Tomas' and Jean's wives there. By this time, they had been told the heartbreaking news about their husbands. Both ladies were camped out on the steps of the Antebellum, mourning and wailing.

Helpless, we sat on the veranda with the leaders, continually praying over the situation. The ministry leaders were immensely upset by the whole ordeal.

Madam J whispered, "It is customary in Haiti, for the family of someone who is seriously injured or killed on *your* property, to hold *you* responsible for the funeral, as well as the care of the spouse and their children."

Tomas' wife screamed loud in Creole, "Oh my God, what's going to happen to me? I have nothing…my husband…he's gone," as she took off running toward the Doctors' Quarters. Throwing herself at the closed gate, she collapsed, as if unplugged.

Jean's pregnant wife had sent a family member for her young children and had been waiting for them while dozing fitfully on the porch. When Tomas' wife screamed and ran, Jean's wife awoke screaming like a victim of a Voo-Doo ritual. She jumped to her feet, trailing behind Tomas' widow, weeping and wailing.

I felt like screaming with them, as my thoughts rolled away like spilled BB pellets. I hugged myself. Jack reached over to touch my back, then we both sat frozen in place.

Thankfully, Vita interpreted from time to time, to help us understand what was happening. Seemingly undaunted, she also took time to fill us in on details.

She said, "The authorities came earlier asking for money to investigate. Then removed the bodies. They claimed some men had climbed the wall onto the property. Then made their way across the grounds and when Jean and Tomas would not unlock the Quarters' gates, the intruders hid, waiting.

Later in the night, the gang scaled the wall onto the stairwell landing. Jean and Tomas must have heard the noise and stepped out of their rooms. They were physically overcome, murdered by machetes."

"Who were these guys?" Tim asked, quieter than usual.

"Polis la (the police) seemed to think they were a band of Aristide supporters."

Aristide was a Haitian politician who became Haiti's first democratically elected president. We were told many people thought he was an evil man, once a Catholic priest that also practiced Voo-Doo. Rumor was that while building the Presidential Palace, he ruthlessly buried a pregnant woman alive under the foyer floors, expecting to receive special voodoo powers. In spite of his wickedness, he had strong followers willing to do anything for him, even murder.

The dark clouds in the Caribbean sky added to an overwhelming sadness. Nerves on edge from the howls and loud moaning settled down after the two grieving widows were brought back to the porch and laid on their pallets. They each whimpered themselves to sleep.

I found myself staring, absorbed in the moment, breathing little prayers.

Bishop J arrived and disappeared upstairs. In a few minutes, Rosa tapped Marilyn, Tim, Jack and me on the shoulder, motioning for us to follow her to the bishop's personal office. One by one, we eased up the stairs, leaving the devastated wives.

We reverently seated ourselves along one side of a folding table, across from Bishop J. His countenance sagged and heavy lines rippled his forehead. I wanted to reach over and pat his arm, to comfort him but held back, lest I disturbed his thoughts.

"How are you doing? Okay?" he began.

We each nodded, mumbling half-reassuring words.

I was full of questions, but asked none.

"News has hit the media about the deaths," Bishop J said, hesitating. "They're saying these men were searching to kill the missionaries staying on our base. Possibly some of my political enemies set this up."

We need to call home and let our families know we are okay.

"The story has reached the United States. Your pastor has called wanting to know, first of all, if his missionaries are okay. I assured him you were fine. He asked if you would like to come home early. He offered to make the necessary arrangements for each of you. What would you like me to tell him?" he concluded.

He looked straight at Tim first. Tim replied, "Yeah, well, with only a few weeks left anyway, I'm thinking that's probably the thing to do."

A light sigh, as he turned to Marilyn, "Oh, yeah, I'm ready to go. We need to get away from here and soon."

And to Jack, who replied, "Yeah, probably."

When his eyes met mine, I paused. Typically not one to make waves, I felt anger rise. My back stiffened and my voice escalated, saying, "Well, you know, the devil didn't send me here, so the devil sure ain't going to run me off. I'd like to stay and finish our work here."

Everyone blinked at me.

Then, right back down the line, Jack replied first, "We're staying!"

Marilyn said, "That's right honey, I'm not going to be run off either."

She faced Tim, who answered, "Hey, you know what, you're right," looking back at Bishop J, he said, "You tell our pastor we are fine and we are going to finish what we started."

Bishop J leaned back in his seat and breathed a smile, the lines lifting in his face. "You are courageous missionaries. It is my pleasure to continue working with you."

I believe his faith had been encouraged. So had ours.

***

Madam J said we'd be safer in Carrefour, so Tim, Jack and I moved the rest of Marilyn's things to our house, while the families of the security guards continued to gather and grieve at Lamintin.

Once we were gone, the elders opened the gates to all the relatives. At great expense, the ministry fed them all. For weeks, the crowds camped out on the grounds, trampling plants and flowers underfoot.

Bathrooms maxed out and broke down.

Our faithful leaders did everything they could to help the families. They agreed to help with travel expenses, and to pay the husbands' salaries for a couple months, to give the wives time to get on their feet. They worked hard to show the Lord's love, while hoping to keep the hounds of bad publicity at bay.

Marilyn helped teach at the Bible School and enjoyed singing with *Light of the World* on the porch in the evenings. Except for jumping wild-eyed at the feedback squeal of a microphone, she was peaceful, talking less and less about that morning.

She loved our young fellas, but her bond was tied to the girls at the Antebellum, and she eventually stopped walking with me to visit the boys.

A week later, after the funeral, she returned to Lamentin.

VBI DINNER

Much like zebras in the wild, after a lion takes one of them down, a zeal of zebra goes back to grazing. So it was after the murder of Jean and Tomas. Life at the base had returned to routine. In the face of possible danger, we had remained.

Without further incident, our international training in Haiti would finish in a couple of weeks.

Marilyn taught one last class at the VBI Bible School. Jack, Tim and I gave her a quick hug, before she caught a TapTap back to Lamentin, thinking we would see her off at the airport in a few days.

She called the next day to tell us goodbye. An opportunity came for her to leave a few days early - the first of us to head home. I would miss her good-natured laugh, healthy hugs, and wise-words-of-life visits.

Tim's departure was in a week, scheduled before he knew our flight plans.

One afternoon, the three of us were sitting on the porch, swatting mosquitoes, filling in names and signing Certificates of Completion for our VBI students. The Director sent word through Tomas, for Brother Tim, Jack and me to, "please come back over to the school." He needed to talk to us.

We had heard he had gotten in trouble for taking us off the base across the other side of the island to see the house for lease and for bringing us to visit another church on Sunday. Talking among ourselves as we walked over, we each figured he wanted to talk to us about it.

As we rounded the corner, a few students waved their hands Haiti-style: hands facing downward, dipping like a bucket on a backhoe for us to come over.

In the center of the courtyard stood a table covered in strips of bright colored paper, and on top, Coca Cola bottles lined in a row, beads of condensation rolling down their sides. Ice cold... Beside them lay a plate of homemade biscuit bread with a dark brown filling inside and little bags of papitas (salted fried banana chips) next to them.

Our farewell dinner came as a great surprise to us and at an even greater cost to our students, but they were beaming with pride.

The VBI director stood chuckling with Jack and Brother Tim about being in on the surprise. Tim wiped at his face and Jack fought back tears, both struggling to stay in the conversation with Pastor F.

Our dear friends grabbed our hands, pulled us into a circle, and one of them prayed a blessing in English over the food. Each then pressed us toward the beautiful spread after a hug, insisting that we eat first.

I savored every bite of the Five-Star meal. Smiling and nodding to each other, teachers and students were breaking bread together, a powerful tribal act in most cultures. The Cola, a special treat, not easily found in Haiti, cooled my body, and helped move the knot down my throat, tears already misty in the corners of my eyes. Our students' lovely sacrifice tenderly touched my soul, along with it a deep ache, realizing we would no longer be with them. I had so much I wanted to say, but I was on overload and could barely speak.

Though we each were unable to empty our hearts with words, the blessing they prayed and the shine in their eyes said that maybe, just maybe, we truly had an impact in their lives.

When we were in Bible school with so many Bible teachers and ministers, in a town full of the same, Jack and I did not feel like very bright lights, often wondering what we had to offer anyone.

Yes, a small lamp would seem insignificant at a well-lit football stadium at dusk. But in the dark of night, even a flicked Bic shines bright and overpowers the darkness.

A student once said to us, "I can't believe you would pay your own money and leave your beautiful country and your families, to come here for us. That is great love."

Jack and I cherished this monumental moment of returned love.

It made it all worthwhile!

THE SEND OFF

The spicy smell of Michelin's scrambled eggs, beans and rice breakfast called us to the dining room.

Brother Tim had been gathering his clothes and personal items since the night before, in between people from the community dropping by to say good bye to the preaching machine. Now he was cramming a few last minute things into his backpack.

After our morning meal, he and Daniel once again poured over last minute plans for the orphanage. Tim handed Daniel all the gourdes, except the ten gourdes needed to depart Haiti, from his pockets with a promised pledge of more. Boom bam boom, he was suddenly gone. Back to just the two of us, the room felt hollow in the absence of this faith filled man.

Next day, Michelin came early to show us her Culinary School certificate of completion for first term. We bragged on her, saying how proud we were, and assured her that after we returned home, we would send tuition money for the second term.

Our next few meals had an extra touch of class, with little green sprigs (like parsley), twisted lemons, or flowered radishes garnishing our plates. *Manje a Gou*, Michelin!

In the afternoon, Michelin returned to the house with her son and daughter, who had been visiting from the mountains, to meet us. She smiled, with mother-eyes sparkling, as she presented her beautiful, well-mannered and well-dressed teens. Like we say in the south, they were spit shined and polished.

When she asked in simple English, if we would pray a blessing over them, Jack immediately jumped to his feet, grinning with joy. "We'd be honored, Michelin," he replied. I don't know how much they understood, but Jack prayed over them, a fervent prayer of blessing and wisdom.

Light of the World continued to come each night, singing passionate worship songs to the Lord, as well as gleaning from our last few days together. Each beat of the drum and melodic voice, captured me to the core; for my husband and for these young folks who loved him so.

We gifted our collection of worship CD's to Paolo, for the group to enjoy.

A pleasant surprise came when, Madam J stopped by the house. With hands folded, she said, "Bishop J and I certainly enjoyed having you with us these few months. We 'ope you had a good time serving in *'aiti*."

We assured her we did.

Apologizing for Bishop J not being able to come, she explained, "He is already in the states and I am leaving to join him, later this afternoon."

"That's fine, we understand. We really appreciate everything you have done for us," said Jack. "Please tell Bishop J for us."

"Maybe we will see you in the states. If you ever come to Tulsa, we would love to have you visit us," I added.

She nodded, "We'll do that, thank you." Then she made an unexpected request. "Edeline's sponsor, who has cared for her since she was a little girl in the orphanage, found out she needs an expensive, special procedure done and has made arrangements for her to fly to Texas. Could Edeline travel as far as Miami with you? And could you make sure she makes her connecting flight to Houston? She leaves on the same flight as you do. "

Without hesitation, Jack and I said in chorus, "Yes, of course she can."

With a quick hug and blessing, she slipped out the door.

All the goodbyes were difficult and emotionally charged. Light of the World was especially tough for Jack, but for me it was the boys. We played one last soccer keep-away-from-Beverly game, and at sunset, flew Mackenzie's' kite as high as we had string for. The little guys were tucked into bed that night with a momma hug and a kiss. On our table, they had left their signed Renoirs, done in crayon.

Later, the older boys rambled into the house. We set chairs in a circle, so we could face one another. One by one, they each stood to say their personal goodbye. Like living Hallmark cards, some had written out their message in English, some spoke through Paolo and some spoke straight from their hearts, of their appreciation of our love for God and for us coming to be with them.

At this point, after trying to remain cool but vibrating with emotion, tears came faster than I could wipe away. I would miss our times together so much and miss seeing their sweet, beautiful faces every day.

When Bebe stood, smiling at me, bravely sharing his heart, I lost it. Tears flooding... Not wanting to embarrass him, I resisted jumping up to hug him, and simply muttered softly, "Thank you, Bebe," forcing my face into a happy smile. He had grown up so much since the beach.

Some of our boys, presented little gifts: a card they had all signed, a wooden cup with our name burnt into it, folded paper flowers, or their hand written messages on scraps of paper.

Jack and I each shared from our heart our love for them, encouraging them in the Lord, and promising to return to take them to the beach, again. They approved, by yelling and stomping their feet. We joined them in the stomping, creating lots of noise and laughter. One at the time, they filed out of the room back to their bunks. No noise, no talking, as if someone had muted us...

Even our neighbor, the "I'm Blessed, I'm Blessed" screaming lady had been calm for a while. Answered prayer!

Balek arrived the next morning to take us to the airport, with Edeline, dressed in a tailored, navy blue gabardine suit. We had an early flight. Like a child, I waved goodbye to the yellow mosquito net, the rodent infested dresser, the cold-dribble-shower, the bare mango trees, the bumpy road, the smelly city and at last, a hug and tearful wave goodbye to Balek.

* * *

We stepped off the plane in Miami, racing to immigration with Edeline. She told us on the plane, that she had never flown before. Nearly kicking the seat in front of her from shear excitement, she reminded me of my first flight.

Like me, she had loved the take-off and the landing. Her mouth flew open as she marveled in flight at her small island country below and later patted my arm, pointing at the clouds, with the sun blasting over them in brilliant colors. "Looks like you could walk across them," she said, eyes gleaming.

Edeline bounced slightly in her seat when the stewardess brought her *free* meal and juice. She pocketed her little pack of peanuts.

But the most amusing thing of all, was in the Miami airport. Edeline stopped dead in front of the escalator. She could not figure out how to mount the thing. I had never thought about how a twenty-two year old adult would feel, trying to ride the moving stairs for the first time. She looked on quizzically, observing others hop aboard, floating downward. This would be a bold move.

We waited patiently, as she watched and thought about it. Jack took her carry-on, so she could hold on with both hands. One quick step and a squeal… We applauded her courage and jumped on behind. Such a small thing, for such a big grin.

After finally maneuvering her and ourselves through the long lines of customs, we directed her toward baggage claim. Luggage reclaimed and reloaded for the connecting flights, and tucking away her passport, Edeline asked, "Do we still have time?"

Her one request, before we separated was to have an American hamburger. Our only option at this point was Burger King. Not indulging ourselves, we sat with her as she yummed and hummed through her first burger, fries and Coke.

Afterward, we hurried her down the long hall toward her gate and asked her to call us when she arrived in Texas. Head held high, she readily boarded the escalator, glancing back with that same big grin.

Having Edeline with us took some of the sting out of our departure. But now, the hand of sentiment that had plucked my heart strings closed around it with a squeeze. I wept.

I tell of my adventure to the Pearl, as a woman, but the desire came about from a young girl's dream, of going into all the world one day, to share the love of the Lord. It's been my privilege to be allowed to love and be loved in a world wrought with hardship and death. At one time, the path my life was headed, it looked impossible.

But Lord, You turned all that around and made a way for me. Thank you!

These times have become a treasure, Jack and I still hold in our heart today.

As water reflects the face, so one's life reflects the heart. Proverbs 27: 19

EPILOGUE

When we returned home to Tulsa, we had no debriefing. No place for emotional decompression. Jack and I did not understand that we needed time to readjust to the American pace, food, smells, temperatures, driving and work schedules. We were home!

Instead, we found ourselves grumpy with each other, not knowing why.

Sometimes Jack walked room to room, as if looking for a lost shoe. Once, I found myself standing in place trying to decide where I wanted to go, and wondering why.

Simple things felt foreign, like planning meals, shopping for groceries but now with multiple choices in clean stores without the need to look over my shoulder or hug my purse quite so tightly, remembering to prepare breakfast, lunch, and dinner; cleaning house and doing laundry; mowing the grass;

taking garbage to the road, bagged and tidy in a container.

Returning to the mundane…

Jack said, "It feels so weird to be driving again." And we marveled together at the flat roadways devoid of dust, rocks and crowds of people walking dangerously close to the edge, no stinky smells wafting through the windows, and we admired smooth entry ramps to well-marked highways built for high speed.

All around me, my friends and co-workers were changed…but of course they were not, I was the different one. I was forever altered, improved and enriched, though it didn't feel like it at the moment.

For weeks, I cried off and on, even at work. Weeping and trying not to judge our American affluence. Reminding myself that that very affluence was what afforded us to be able to go to countries like Haiti to help.

Jack and I were in culture shock in our own country!

Years later, I learned and understood that adults debriefed *best* by reflecting with other adults, which we had desperately needed. Eventually, time and prayer brought peacefulness.

But I did not want to forget what I had seen.

In due time, we excitedly returned to Haiti. Several trips, in fact… We always met with *our boys* taking them to the beach again, as promised.

One Christmas, we brought a group of six people bearing gifts: toys for the little ones, watches for the older boys. Our team helped Jack and me purchase ceiling fans for each of the boys' dorm rooms. We mounted the fans and painted walls. The boys *helped*, until we realized their beautiful black faces and hands were now pale blue, yellow and green. Dripping paint brushes and rollers, slopped by their shoes, left mixed-colored trails from room to room.

Naomi, a team member, and I cleaned up the smaller children and took them outside to play. Jack and his buddy Marion, taught the older boys, who loved to learn new things, how to wire the fans and the art of painting.

In the summer, we revisited the boys. Noticing their lack of toys, we asked where they were. Several of them told us the toys had been taken from them after we left. (Possibly sold, we were told…) That somehow didn't seem right and was not only disappointing, but quite upsetting.

We had returned with our church to help host a large open-air meeting at the soccer stadium in Carrefour. Jack and I never mentioned to the team that they were staying at Doctors' Quarters, where the murders had taken place just two years before. The stairwell's archway, now dressed in decorative wrought iron, prevented outside entry.

Jack preached in the large open air meetings, along with our Pastor. I was one of the teachers at the women's conference with thousands attending. My friend Deborah J, after hearing our Haiti stories in the class we taught at VBI Tulsa, came on this trip.

A classy lady of means, Deborah chose to ride with me on 50 lb. bags of beans in the back of Balek's truck, to see our beloved boys. She was thrilled. How wonderful it felt to know that our trip to Haiti had impacted her and her husband to later travel to many countries, helping various missionaries for several years.

Daniel and Maribel married and started Daniel's Orphanage. As promised, Tim raised the money, not only to set them up but also to sponsor them monthly. It lasted for a few years, until Tim, feeling the money was not being used the way they had agreed, eventually pulled out his support.

We personally, sent money to Michelin for a required hand mixer and for her tuition to culinary school for the next two years. On one of our return trips, we asked around about Michelin, but no one seemed to know where she went or what she was doing. Our prayer is that she is, at least, making a good living for herself and her family.

Marilyn became involved in a missions ministry in North Carolina for a few years until finally leaving for the Congo, as originally planned. As she was flying over Africa she prayed, "Lord, why me?" She heard in her heart, "Because I knew you would do it."

A few years later, Edeline, her husband and little boy came to visit Marilyn in Nashville, Tennessee. Marilyn told me on the phone, "Edeline never had to have surgery for the brain tumor. When the doctors rechecked her, there was only an indention on the bone where the tumor once laid.

The headaches had stopped and her menstrual cycle had restarted."

Glory to God for Edeline's healing!

Jack and I worked for the next four years at the Victory Bible Institute, VBI in Tulsa. Jack as the Off-Campus Coordinator and I as the Office Manager, then later as the International Student Advisor.

Through that role, I learned the requirements to bring a student into the country.

Obed, the 26-year-old orphan that interpreted for us, had stayed in touch, wanting to come to VBI Tulsa. We agreed to sponsor him for the school's two-year program. Through a series of amazing events, Obed was allowed to come and live with us. It's difficult to get out of Haiti because Haitians tend not to return.

One day, I will share his miraculous story.

And Balek? Obed told us a few years later, that Balek had died in a car crash. My heart ached for his precious family's loss and longed to, once again, see that big smile of his.

Haiti, The Pearl is a valuable study of culture with its charming, interesting people. A Living Pearl. But to visit her, one must be prepared emotionally to experience difficult things; like the ever present hunger, cruelty, deprivation, lack, and death. *Oh, so much death!*

Our hopes were raised for the Pearl, when we met a young married, Haitian man in Tulsa, full of enthusiasm, who thought he might one day return and run for president of Haiti. He had great vision and dreams for his country. But he told us, logistically, even if he started today, it would be ten years before the most basic of infrastructure would be in place.

Regrettably, his life situation changed and his lack of financial backing put a stop to the whole idea.

Earthquakes, storms and floods have since ravaged Haiti. Vast amounts of money were poured into that tiny country. Leaders we have spoken to say that the funds sent after one particular storm, something like $9 million, were not properly managed and no one seems to know where the money went. The people of Haiti benefitted little. It seems perhaps someone's purse did. Like pockets with holes in them...

Jack and I have not returned to Haiti for many years now, but continue to pray for her. Maybe one day, one of our boys or one of the girls, will rise up to bring the living Pearl to her once radiant life, restoring her original grandeur.

Lord, as You have proven over and over to me, not even that is impossible with You.

Our boys enjoying their Caribbean Sea

Made in the USA
Columbia, SC
13 September 2018